FATHER MAURICE NÉDONCELLE was
born in Roubaix, France, in 1905. He
attended St. Sulpice Seminary and the
Sorbonne. He has received Doctorates in
Philosophy and Letters from the Sorbonne
and a Doctorate in Theology from the University of Strasbourg (France).

He is currently Dean and Professor of
Fundamental Theology at the Catholic
Theological Faculty of the University of
Strasbourg, posts he has held since 1945.
Previously Father Nédoncelle taught phi-
losophy at the Catholic University of Lille.

His main interest has been in philosophy,
especially contemporary schools of phenomenology, existentialism and personalism. In
addition Father Nédoncelle has written extensively on the history of English thought
in the seventeenth and nineteenth centuries.

GOD'S ENCOUNTER WITH MAN

GOD'S ENCOUNTER WITH MAN

A Contemporary Approach to Prayer

MAURICE NÉDONCELLE

*Dean of the Faculty of Theology
at Strasbourg University*

SHEED AND WARD : NEW YORK

This translation of Prière humaine prière divine
(*Editions Desclée de Brouwer*) was made by A. MANSON

NIHIL OBSTAT: JOANNES M. T. BARTON, S.T.D., L.S.S.
CENSOR DEPUTATUS
IMPRIMATUR: PATRITIUS CASEY
VICARIUS GENERALIS
WESTMONASTERII: DIE 4a JUNII 1964

The Nihil obstat *and* Imprimatur *are a declaration that a book
or pamphlet is considered to be free from doctrinal or moral
error. It is not implied that those who have granted the* Nihil
obstat *and* Imprimatur *agree with the contents, opinions or
statements expressed.*

Published in England under the title
The Nature and Use of Prayer.

French text © 1962 by Desclée de Brouwer
English translation © 1964 by Burns & Oates Ltd
and Sheed & Ward, Inc.

Library of Congress Catalog Card Number 64-19898

Manufactured in the United States of America

Contents

Preface

The subject of the first part of this book is prayer addressed to men, and that of the second, prayer addressed to heaven.

No phenomenological study of prayer between human beings has really been made. This omission is regrettable. Men pray to each other throughout their lives, and the study of a fact of this sort enables us to realise that there is here an unknown but essential sphere of anthropology. Moreover, although this fact is not apparently religious (except in the case of idolatry), it forms one of the indispensable starting-points for religion. That this is so cannot be understood without this preliminary analysis, which itself, it is surprising to observe, can be of use to the theologian. Most of the concepts and methods of the praying soul that turns to God are already present in the movement in which we turn towards our fellows. But, of course, the change in the horizon is radical, and one of our main tasks here will be to discover the difference that lies behind the superficial sameness.

We shall adopt a phenomenological approach, i.e. we shall try to describe prayer as it manifests itself in mankind with its essential tendencies. But, as such a description might well be too lengthy and indeed prove impossible if we should try to cover every civilisation and every age, we shall be content with our own phenomenology, that is, with the experience which we can gain of these things as men of the West, living in the twentieth century, heirs of a Christian and Graeco-Roman tradition. This will not, however, exclude occasional reference to other kinds of experience.

Above all, it will not be so narrowly conceived as to banish a true philosophy or theology of prayer. Our aim has been to describe, but to do so without concealing our convictions. It would be extremely artificial, in a book of this kind, to put essences on one side and concrete existences on the other. Furthermore, there are regions that cannot be discovered and understood without first choosing a road and deciding that it is the right one. Finally, the experience to be described is not always an emotion that is felt; it can be a truth that is verified.

According to Joseph de Maistre, the value of a civilisation depends upon the quality and forms of prayer that men offer to God. Arnold Toynbee, in our day, comes very close to this thesis: "The Abba Pater addressed to the transcendent God forms the only certain foundation for complete brotherhood among men".[1] He even calculates that the chances of survival for a nation depend upon its religious ideal. The inferior forms of prayer, for example, those of a nationalist and militarist piety, seem to him destined to bring to destruction any system of life nourished on a spirituality of this kind. This provocative statement cannot be proved over only a very short space of time and is no doubt debatable, but it is based on a correlation that is certain: just as men pray to God starting from an experience of prayer between themselves, so their way of praying to God cannot be without effect upon their mutual intercourse and on their way of working out their common destiny.

The reader will not find an exhaustive analysis in these pages; we hope, however, that they will provide him with a stimulus to reflection. We have examined the main avenues and cleared some of the thickets. It is open to anyone to continue the exploration.

[1]Cf. the report by H. I. Marrou in the review *Esprit*, July 1952, p. 122.

Part One

PRAYER AS FROM MAN TO MAN

CHAPTER I

Preliminaries

1. The Domain of the Vocative

Prayer belongs to the domain of the vocative, and the vocative is
one of the basic functions of the mind.[1] This is amply proved by
comparative grammar. No language exists whose structure is not
profoundly influenced in many ways by its mention of other people,
and, more directly, by the forms in which other people are addressed.
The conjugations and personal pronouns or adjectives, of course,
always bear this mark, a fact that hardly needs further demonstration.[2]

There is an undoubted tendency in man to conceal any idea of
summoning others to act. We attempt this concealment by directing
attention to the objective façade in the questions we put to others.
Instead of saying: "Would you be good enough to show me the
road to Taunton?", we merely say: "Which is the road to Taunton?" The question mark absolves us from the introductory formula,
or even from the "please", which courtesy still compels us to use
sometimes in dialogue. (Conscience provokes remorse for our very
real indifference to the man we are questioning.) In fact everything
proceeds as though questions and answers had no connexion with
any individual and formed an autonomous mode of intercourse. The

---

[1] The vocative form of address is part of the wider activity of questioning. A
question may express a doubt or an appeal. Note that L. H. Gray, *Foundations
of Language*, New York, 1939, would prefer to connect address with exclamation
—a debatable point of view.

[2] L. H. Gray makes a distinction, in Indo-European and Semitic languages,
between the *base* and the *inflexion* of words. But the base, obtained by removing
every element of inflexion, seems to him identical with the structure of address as
we find it in two forms: (1) the imperative of the second person singular in
active verbs (*age*, in Latin); and (2) the vocative singular of the noun (*domine*).
The base would seem to have no other absolute use (op. cit., pp. 150, 192).

art of economising in words and of pretending that the persons of the speakers may be discounted, becomes extremely complex and ingenious when the content of discourse concerns external nature or individuals other than those engaged in the dialogue. The publication of a book provides a perfect example of a kind of disengagement all round. The author and the purchaser (or reader) do not address one another. The publisher comes between them and picks up their exchanges off-stage. The book is a source of information from which anyone can draw at will. Its title and table of contents help to produce an indirect encounter between writer and reader, and thus relieve them of the necessity of establishing a living contact. All the means of communication which we use in our daily activities take the same short cuts while keeping the interlocutors apart.

Even where the bodies or the minds of two given speakers are concerned the play of question and answer often becomes automatic. "How are you?" "All right; how are you?" are exchanges which make no demand upon our personal attention; they are performed by the robot who functions in each one of us. Japanese goes even further in this direction; its tendency is to obliterate the persons confronting each other, even when the sphere of automatic response has to be left behind and when concrete decisions have to be taken. In Japanese it is not merely the grammatical use of the first person that is disliked; any reference at all to a person is avoided if it can possibly be concealed without causing confusion in practical behaviour. Thus we find impersonal phrases such as: "A short walk would give pleasure." Only the actual situation can clarify the equivocal expression and determine whether it is to me or to you or to someone else that the words are addressed. Such reserve is not altogether absent from the West. Sometimes the depersonalisation is in the interests of speed: "A cigarette?" and, in this case, a gesture makes the meaning plain. Sometimes it is more subtle, almost oriental, as in anonymous invitations: "Mrs X. At Home on Thursday at 3 p.m.", though it is true that the person invited is addressed on the envelope.

In all these procedures the avoidance of the vocative is more apparent than real. Indeed, the impersonal style of a regulation or reprimand is a means of intimidation, for anyone may feel that *he* is really the person envisaged and, therefore, arbitrarily exposed to punishment. A distinction should be made between a concealed approach to another and an approach that is slanted. The latter has much narrower implications and its aim is quite different. An apostrophe may be slanted towards the first person plural ("And how are we today?"), or—more commonly—towards the third person ("And how is Mr Jones today?"), or, lastly, it may be a compromise between the third and second person ("Your Grace"). This procedure has become so firmly adopted in Italian, German and other languages, that it has led to the substitution of the personal pronouns of the third person for those of the second (Lei, Sie, etc.). This way of speaking, originating in the reverential fear of a vassal for his lord, has now been released from its aristocratic confines and become democratic. Its form has become reciprocal, and marks the worth of individuals independently of any class structure. It is the sign that every individual has come to be accepted as significant. Language thus used has put on court dress but, in certain circumstances, every man may make it his own. Every citizen has the right to formal respect from others. The procedure has nothing in common with the Japanese practice noted above; far from concealing persons, it emphasises their uniqueness. The same might be said of the words formerly used to conclude a letter: "Your humble and obedient servant", or even of the modern phrase: "Yours sincerely". The humble ego is a mere satellite of the "thou" round which it circles.

The vocative is a mode that admits of two extremes. One of these is command, the other is declaration. A command is intended to produce either a reflex action or a spontaneous submission of the will, antecedent to any thought about it. It is like an echo, in the realm of ideas and speech, of the creative act which brings a being into existence out of nothingness. But it is a very weak echo, and it quickly encounters the hesitation or the resistance of wills that have been created before it, and that are perfectly capable of directing their own lives. That is why it makes a deliberate effort to reduce them to their original plasticity; it is not conservative, it is retrograde. Often it is helped by a natural mechanism which intervenes between the command and the deed to be done. This mechanism of obedience is emotion, emotion which is primarily fear; it corresponds, on the part of the subject, to the anger by means of which the commander maintains his command. Should that fail, there is always constraint. Constraint, in fact, is implicit in a command. Diplomacy, on the other hand, is practically a denial of any right to command, or, if not quite that, it transforms the command into a mixed method of approach.

Ultimatums are sometimes issued in a courteous form, or addressed with respect to those concerned, but forms recognising another person's freedom are rare.[3] They may indeed be an expression of a conflict of functions hard to reconcile, a conflict that may well give rise to entirely honourable conscientious difficulties. Apart from this, however, it is to be feared that the politeness of the command, more often than not, hides a strong element of hypocrisy or weakness. The purpose of a command is to get something done immediately, something either physical or intellectual. Of course, the discipline may have been freely accepted beforehand; but the formal structure of a command, as distinct from a prayer, necessitates that freedom shall not be taken into account. It would be foolish and disastrous for a superior to go down on his knees before his subordinates. All one may hope for and expect from him is that he will command with the intention to educate, i.e. that his purpose will be to use authority to *create* freedom—and so to enable himself to be dispensed with.[4]

---

[3] In this case, from a linguistic point of view, they derive their disguise not from the imperative but from other moods, and approach the forms used for the first or third person. "Strictly speaking, the imperative has but one person, the second singular active, and denotes only a *positive command*. The other persons are drawn, for the most part, either from the injunctive (e.g., Sanskrit *sárpatu*= Greek ἑρπέτω= Latin *serpitō* 'let him creep!') . . . or from the subjunctive (e.g., Sanskrit *sárpāni* 'let me creep!' cf. Greek ἕρπωμεν 'let us creep!'). Very frequently, *prohibitions* are expressed, not by the imperative, but by other moods (e.g., Latin *serpe* 'creep!' is a real imperative, but *ne serpas* 'don't creep!' is a subjunctive)." L. H. Gray, op. cit., p. 209.

[4] Both command and obedience must be distinguished from the motives that prompt them, or, *a fortiori*, from the general reasons which move us to enter the field of their activity. Here we are only concerned with what is sheerly essential

At the opposite extremity of the domain of the vocative, there is the simple declaration made to another. The speaker provides information—and nothing more—either about himself, or about the person he is speaking to, or about other persons or events. A declaration is definitely an inter-subjective phenomenon; it is not just a monologue; it is meant to be heard, even if by no one in particular. Though it be spoken to empty space, it is intended to be not a meditation but an address. It may, of course, happen that an audience has in fact slipped away and the speaker failed to perceive it, or anyhow appeared not to perceive it. This does not affect the essential nature of a declaration. The fact is that declaration, as such, is not concerned with what others feel about it; in fact, other people, as people reacting to one another, are largely irrelevant, provided they hear what one has to say to them, like, for example, the colourless confidants of the French classical theatre.[5]

Nevertheless, between the two extremes of command and declaration, there is a minimum in common; a command is, in its own way, a piece of information; a declaration simply asks that its making should be noted, and in doing this compels attention. Moreover, a declaration is not always a sequence of unconnected statements; it may be expressed as an argument, and thus exercise a kind of higher constraint, that of objective evidence. With these reservations, we may say that the only purpose of information is to make its content plain. It is indifferent to everything besides this and is unconcerned with any behaviour of other people which it may set in motion, still less with their personalities. It has no prescience, and contains a kind of scientific purity, a generosity of mind which is content to transmit and ask for nothing in return. At least, that is what it is

in them and with their function isolated from any other consideration. In the concrete exercise of authority, other things besides this essence fortunately come into play.

[5] The mental attitude analysed above has obviously nothing in common except the word, with a "declaration of love" or a "declaration of war". But even in these instances the phrase is not inapt, the lover who "declares" his love, the statesman who "declares" war, is bringing into the open something already existing, confronting others with an undeniable reality, and communicating information in such a way as to make it clear that a point of no return has been reached. How they will accept it and deal with it is a different matter.

essentially, before it becomes degraded into routine behaviour without meaning. For some people end up by talking to themselves alone. When words issue from a speaker like semi-conscious breathing their only use is to make the neighbours laugh.

2. *The Place of Prayer in the Domain of the Vocative*

The place of prayer lies between these two extremes. It is not a command, for it does not find its origin in the requirement that others should fall into line, nor even in the authoritative creation of a dependent ego. It comes in after the beginning, when the ego to which it speaks has already grown up to independence and can act with freedom. Prayer accepts the fact that it may not be heard, whereas a command cannot admit refusal, for that would imply its complete negation. On the other hand, prayer is not merely a declaration, for it is not indifferent to the person to whom it is addressed. A man who prays needs more than a listening ear; he needs a face turned towards him and deeds done. He is not simply transmitting a message; he is waiting for an answer.

We will now scrutinise these different points more closely.

(1) If we except the border-line case of an administrative request, prayer is *contemplative*, and it is this, as we have just noted, that distinguishes it from a declaration. It needs a personal presence.

This characteristic is evident even in those mixed forms that are still very close to a declaration—praise or insult given directly to the person concerned.[6] But although a panegyrist or a practitioner of abuse desires the presence of the man who has provoked him, the man's freedom is treated as a trifle. A prayer, however, in the strict sense, cannot afford to disregard it; it wants a person and wants him free. When Andromache begs Hector not to go out to battle, she implores him for their son's sake, for his sake and for hers; she knows she has little chance of being heard, but she feels that there is just one chance and she takes it: "'Hector,' she said, 'you are possessed.

---

[6] Blessings and curses complicate matters because they are prayers addressed to invisible powers *in the presence of* the man, rather than speeches directed to him. He is intended to be a witness of the sacred esteem or hatred in which he is held.

This bravery of yours will be your end. You do not think of your little boy or your unhappy wife, whom you will make a widow soon. Some day the Achaeans are bound to kill you in a massed attack.'"[7] She would not have prayed to Hector had he been a mere abstract principle or an inflexible law. She believes he can be influenced and that he has not yet made an irrevocable decision. The contemplation involved in prayer is, therefore, active; it is bound to cause some change either in you or in me. Hector would not give in, so it was Andromache who had to change her mind; her withdrawal and her tears reveal this indirectly.

Prayer is a form of contemplation which usually has to deal with the obstacle of distance; even so, it is never uttered in a night so dark that the person to whom it is addressed is completely inaccessible. Absolute agnosticism at once causes prayer to wither because it destroys the elementary possibility of contemplation. There must be at least the face remembered and hoped for, even when that face is there no more. Someone may pick up the bottle thrown into the sea and bring the news home. And what would we not give to see this messenger before we drown!

Contemplation distinguishes a prayer from a declaration. Contemplation, however, is never the only factor; it is one element in prayer, but prayer also entails petition and devotion.

(2) Because it is a *petition*, prayer cannot be a command. As soon as I "pray" another person, even in an imperative mode ("I beg you to stop"), I renounce the use of constraint; if only for a time, I reject violence. I want to obtain something from him, rather than to subject him to something. I accept his being as a centre of activity and responsibility. But I go further, I abstain from giving him what could really be called an order. I tone down my command and am content to exhort him. And even an exhortation that is vehement presupposes freedom. Prayer takes care not to overstep the boundary and trespass into the realm of command. It is related to rhetoric (itself of the family of dialectic or the "art of dialogue"), not to abstract logic which would leave no room for unexpected

---

[7] *Iliad*, 6, 407-10. [Trans. E. V. Rieu, Penguin Classics, p. 128.]

contingencies; it is a discourse between one centre of freedom and another. Even if my shout were irrepressible and the person to whom I called for help the only one on the bank who could save me, I still should not be saved if he refused to jump into the water. An SOS is a prayer from a person in danger, although the obligation to help him may be an imperative of conscience or the law.

The superior who meets with resistance grows angry and induces fear. The man who prays discards this emotional resource and appeals to pity, like Priam before Achilles: "'Most worshipful Achilles,' he said, 'think of your own father.'"[8] Thereupon begins a whole scale in the methods of persuasion. Priam clasps Achilles' knees, the seat of power. He retains his dignity, even though Hector's corpse has not been burnt and Hector suffers because his *psyche* has not yet been freed. "Achilles, fear the gods, and be merciful to me, remembering your own father, though I am even more entitled to compassion, since I have brought myself to do a thing that no one else on earth has done—I have raised to my lips the hand of the man who killed my son."[9] Achilles, too, retains his dignity, though with a great effort: "Do not exasperate me now, sir, when I have enough already on my mind, or I may break the laws of Zeus and, suppliant though you are, show you as little consideration as I showed Hector in my huts."[10] But how often do the partners, in the *Iliad* and elsewhere, fall below the level of this scene! There are petitions that grovel in abjection and flattery; there are replies that lacerate and kill. Then prayer goes sour in the depths of the soul. If, however, it ascends, it strips off the gear of seduction and no longer tries to deceive or to stir up pity. It asks and receives in joy, it has become the prayer of mutual love and friendship: Achilles and Patroclus.

Even when, in itself, it is a pitiable thing, petition cannot discard the nobility which contemplation confers on it: it creates a spiritual bond between one man and another. It does not take us out of the realm of material things, since it presupposes a perception of physical gestures by the other, but it does lead to an exchange of spiritual

[8] *Iliad*, 24, 486. [Rieu, p. 450.]   [9] Ibid., 477 ff., p. 450.
[10] Ibid., 568–70, p. 452.

states of mind through the intermediaries of sight and hearing. When I give an order, I am already in this kingdom of speech and sight, but the order still contains a threat of physical violence. When I adopt an attitude of prayer, I dismiss all thought of such bodily intervention, even as a last resort, and I enter into a series of relationships in which mental life can develop indefinitely without contact. This indeed is the special characteristic of personal and interpersonal knowledge. The knowledge of nature also requires this initial privilege conferred on the eye and ear; but it demands a considerable number of verifications through contact, whereas the reflexions of conscience and its communications with others can arise at any moment on the basis of the simple sensory perceptions of sight and hearing.

This state of affairs—which, to begin with, is that of prayer between men—is admirably symbolised by the grille through which we see and hear in the parlours of enclosed convents: these women lead an existence in which sight and sound are the only means of communication. Of course, the relations between persons are not limited to such monastic discipline; they often involve contact and handling. Moreover, life lived through sight and sound is still a material reality. And yet the ego and its fellows subsist and develop at a level not reached by the activities of touch which are essential for any effect we desire to have on nature. I never "pray" to nature in order to effect a change in it; I submit it to a technique, and techniques are not compatible with the relinquishing of methods that involve physical contact. Prayer is the most significant form, the most striking example of purposeful thought, based only on the data supplied by the eye and ear.

Against this, we may be reminded that Priam clasped Achilles' knees. And who would deny the historical importance of the kissing of feet by supplicants, or of the clasping of hands? A command keeps bodies apart more drastically. But, in reality, a command marks out distances as a warning against any attempt at supplication, and as a hint that if it becomes necessary, the recalcitrant body will soon be seized upon and made ready to obey willy-nilly. There is nothing like this in the contacts between a man who prays and the person who accepts the prayer. A petition admits the possibility of contact only very tactfully, i.e. it always accepts the possibility that the body of the person addressed may be withdrawn. When a kiss is necessary, a petition contains an element of seduction; it is, if not downright impure, at least less than perfect, for though its perfection may not entail dispensing with a kiss, it does entail the ability to do without it.

(3) Lastly, prayer is *devotion*; it backs up the request with a gift. An external or interior pledge is given to the person to whom the prayer is addressed. Every prayer contains an offering and even a sacrifice. We inconvenience ourselves, we give up something, and what we give up we offer to the other person. It is the impulse to offer oneself that really matters; the movement begins from within. When this inner movement is made manifest by the yielding up of some material possession, the renunciation becomes symbolical, and, therefore, the manner of giving is more important than the gift itself. The inconvenience resulting from the deprivation—and the danger involved in committing oneself—react joyfully upon the initial act of offering and prevent it from being a mere murmur of empty words. Some self-effacement is thus bound up with prayer. We do not prefer the other person's will to our own by any absolute necessity, for we may hope to change it, but we bring something of our own activity or possessions to him, and we offer it in homage.

And yet, even when a prayer is accompanied by a promise of obedience, it is still not the same thing as obedience; it is directed towards a different purpose. The two acts may be connected; they are not identical. It follows, *a fortiori*, that the purpose of prayer is not self-destruction, but self-affirmation, sometimes expressed with vehemence, before another human being. Prayer is not suicide, nor is suicide a prayer.

When we are considering the problem of a return to nothingness, we should distinguish two forms of it: spontaneous dissolution and voluntary self-sacrifice. There are people whose individuality seems to dissolve like snow in the sun, when confronted by certain others. Their servility is antecedent to any deliberation and comes into play as by instinct, or like a hypnotic sleep. In such cases one feels that the relationship between human beings is a copy of what exists between the members of a wolf-pack in which the leader's prestige enables him to impose his law on the other animals. This natural phenomenon seems to survive in the grovelling humility of the slave, or the shouts of the party member paying hysterical worship to his chief. Prayer is incompatible with this sort of disintegration which, it may be said, does not leave one a leg to stand on. To stifle one's reason is not to pray.

The case of the man who gives his life after due thought, voluntarily, involves a more difficult problem. Is this not, after all, the purest type of self-sacrifice there is? For even though, *ex hypothesi*, the deliberate surrender of bodily life for the sake of another makes it impossible to continue the prayer that had been begun, it would still seem to be a fulfilment and perfect achievement of prayer as well as of personality. But, though it may be necessary to throw oneself into the fire to save another person's life, it can never be necessary to surrender the loftiest functions of the mind for the sake of anyone; the abdication of the will would make nonsense of the act of love. To repudiate the basic values of the self is not a virtue; it is a perversion and, ultimately, an impossibility.

Petition and devotion are always implied in contemplation and these three elements of prayer are inseparable. But the part played by each of them constantly varies. To ask and to give seem to be contrary and opposed activities. And yet, as soon as the level of prayer rises, the ratio ceases to be one of inverse proportion. For then it is no longer something material that is asked for, but the presence of a person whom it is delightful to contemplate. One is ready to give everything for the presence: "See me more often and give me nothing."[11] Petition and devotion outgrow their separateness and fuse in a desire for a communion of mind and heart. Moreover, they are never practised in a night so dark that contemplation is ruled out.

Still, contemplation does carry with it a respect for the freedom of the person to whom we are praying—and he may choose to with-

[11] Racine, *Bérénice*, Act II, Scene IV.

draw. The souls of those who pray are exposed to the tragedies of absence. An attempt may be made to escape the impact of a later absence by taking refuge in the memory of an earlier presence, but this is only a makeshift, for it leads to the soul's imprisonment in an imagination; a picture of the other person is created which may not resemble what he is really like, or may represent something less than he really is. Prayer among human beings often becomes unilateral and thus loses its true nature. But it is never entirely solitary to begin with, and it is possible for the original picture to be developed without becoming inevitably untrue.

At the beginning of this chapter we noted that praise and insult are equidistant from declaration and prayer. What we have just said about devotion illustrates a different aspect: praise can also be a form of devotion to another person, and an insult may be inverted devotion, the other person being contemplated with hatred. In that case a man will expend his substance and his being in order to promote either the happiness or the affliction of his partner.

3. How Prayer fits into Natural Destiny

In prayer between human beings there is always an external element affecting the relationship between the person praying and the other to whom the prayer is addressed.

We will take another look at the wonderful passage in the *Iliad* which has already provided us with an example, the passage in which Andromache tries in vain to convince Hector. She realises at once that she has to meet the opposing will of her husband, and also the situation in which he finds himself. She has an obscure sense of that factor which he mentions several times: the weight of destiny. He is bound to take into account the army, the people, the position he himself has to fill, the intolerable shame he would experience if he ran away from the battle, etc. All this is a manifold expression of a necessity inherent in events and which leads him to death. His love of Andromache is not disputed; he recalls it and proclaims it to be above every other attachment. But he is not free to push aside his fate. And even should he try to do this, he would still lose his honour, and this is subject to conditions which are not his to dispose of; he would blemish the conjugal love he cherishes; he would no longer be able to respect himself, nor could his wife continue to respect him; she would have nothing better than a traitor to love.[12]

The intervention of destiny, or, of cosmic determinism, if the phrase is preferred, in a prayer addressed to another, and in the answer he is led to make, restricts the area of possibility. The dialogue between Hector and Andromache is dominated by this conviction, and when Hector interrupts his replies in order to invoke Zeus, he does not ask the father of the gods for his life; that would have seemed to him chimerical and impious. He considers that the only contingency on which Zeus himself can bring his good will to bear is the future of Astyanax. Accordingly he prays to the god on behalf of his son. Some commentators hold that destiny is the consequence of an oath: Zeus cannot unsay his words; the die is cast. This does not really affect the matter; when a mortal is being considered, his destiny is determined by invisible powers, like a piece of cloth whose threads were combined when life began. Greek wisdom expressed this situation by a metaphor less rigid than our scientific determinism; the intertwined threads allow for some adjustment, slight though it be. Thus Achilles

[12] This theme, no more than implicit in the *Iliad*, is present in all subsequent literature down to Claudel's *Satin Slipper*, e.g. in the classics of seventeenth-century France:
Corneille, *Le Cid*, Act III, Scene IV:
"She who loved me noble, would hate me dishonoured";
Horace, Act IV, Scene VII:
"Are you so deadly an enemy to my honour, that you would be glad to see me covered with shame?";
Polyeucte, Act II, Scene II:
"A sense of duty less firm and less sincere would not have deserved great Severus' love".
And in Racine's *Bérénice*, Act V, Scene VI:
"You yourself would blush at my coward's behaviour;
You would be ashamed to see, following in your train,
An unworthy emperor".
The opposite point of view is more rarely expressed. But in a ludicrous tragedy of the eighteenth century, *Cocatrix*, by Collé, it is expressed in a very decisive way. The hero Amatrox says to Vortex, his intimate friend and accomplice: "I love you the more, the less I esteem you." Only in contemporary immoralist literature has "I love you the *more*" become "I love you the *better*".

has the choice between a long life of mediocrity and a short life of glory.

We reach the conclusion which holds good quite apart from Homeric beliefs: prayer between human beings has only an enclosed area to move in. We are in the world, *Dasein* compels us to accept a whole system of restraints. Some form what Jaspers would call boundary situations, common to all men, others are strictly individual; some are permanent, others are passing; some are due to nature or society, others are the inheritance of our own earlier deeds; some are absolute, others may in a measure be relaxed. The will of a hero has full play in the sphere allocated to it, but that will has a bridle. Its freedom is not unqualified. Neither the petitioner nor the one who answers him can cross the limits that no man may cross. They cannot, while they live, be rid of life. They cannot so spiritualise their relationship that it becomes immaterial, an exchange between two centres of disembodied freedom. Prayer and its answer have their place *within* a destiny, a destiny that implacably settles the boundaries of the dialogue between the two persons concerned.

CHAPTER 2

The Content of Prayer as an Expression of the Bond between Persons

1. The Material Content

Prayer made by one human being to another springs from the urgency of some physiological, psychological or social need. Need forms the material content of prayer, a need that is dominant, at least for the moment. This does not mean, however, that it is always utilitarian in the economic sense, or even that it denotes some immaterial advantage, such as esteem or renown: "Passer-by, tell the Lacedaemonians that we lie here because we obeyed their orders." For some contents are unrelated to any advantage to the petitioner; this is the case when intercession is made for a third person. Others express some wish for the person to whom the request is made and are wholly disinterested; and some indicate an offering that involves pain endured in order to save a loved one from his own vices: "If you wish, add my life to the freedom you have taken from me, provided that the people be not angered by my death and take from you what has cost me so much."[1]

In short, there are contents of prayer that do not exclusively involve self-love, i.e. that are without egoism. The relation between the content and the petitioner is not inevitably the result of either self-interest or disinterested love. It arises simply from desire, from urgent need, as an expression of the personality.

In order to classify the different contents in relation to their subjects, the following possibilities may be distinguished:

(1) If the content is alien to the subjects as such, prayer is functional, not personal. It should not then be called prayer in the strict

[1] Racine, *Britannicus*, Act IV, Scene II.

sense. The *request* addressed to the mayor by a citizen, or to the telephone exchange by a subscriber, is an example of this. I am not acting formally as a man, but as a citizen or a subscriber. And the administration replies in the same style; the departmental head does not react as an individual, but as an anonymous employee. Another might well be substituted for him. The law in particular is prone to personify human relationships. It then arranges them in categories and includes in these categories not only the area of national administration, but even such spheres of private intercourse as may be regarded as institutional. Thus there are forms for official applications, and also for wills, business advertisements, limited companies, etc. An inventory of requests and of the way they are codified could be drawn up according to this principle, and to this would have to be added the enormous mass of additional matter supplied by custom. When we reach the extreme limit, the content gives the impression of being entirely independent of any real, living men and women. "After 10 p.m., you are requested to give your name to the night porter." "Guests are requested not to smoke in the dining room." Guests, smokers, night porters come and go—the notices remain. In the end no one knows who is speaking to whom. If the request is unnoticed or unobserved, no one feels personally insulted. The offence (unless committed with deliberate malice) injures no one in particular; it belongs to that abstract class known as a misdemeanour.

(2) In other cases, there is an accidental connexion with the subjects; I should call this *prayer-as-prattle*. A child who asks his father for a horse, a castle, a car, etc., knows very well that his father won't give it to him. That doesn't matter, it fills up the time spent walking, and, who knows, one day or other, the request may be granted. . . . It should be noted, however, that a very important cleavage has been produced both within the petitioner's attitude and within the actual content of his prayer. On the one hand, the details have no real relationship with his inner self; they engross the conversation and yet are not taken seriously. On the other hand, there is a less obtrusive and more solid content which forms the essence of the prayer: "Father, I trust you, you are my protector. Even though you

refuse to gratify my whims, I know you listen to your child and that you do not fail to appreciate which of his wants may be granted." A child who stamps because he has been refused a toy fully realises that he is not so unfortunate as his tantrums assert. The really forsaken child knows there is nothing to be gained by making a nuisance of himself and so is less noisy.

(3) There are cases in which the content of the prayer symbolically involves a relationship between the minds and hearts of those concerned. What takes place between them is dramatic. The symbolism of the sign may indeed rest upon some apparently insignificant material basis: the gift of a flower, the movement of a hand, a letter of approval—that may be the kind of thing that constitutes the object of the request. Prattle, again, we may say, but, in fact, a new element of significance has intervened and even perhaps a kind of tacit agreement between those concerned, with the material object as the go-between. This is true, *a fortiori*, when the object requested is identical with the content of the request, and when past, present and future are fused in the action: here is Hector whom Achilles killed; this is his body; will he restore it to Priam, or not? The cleavage in this case is very serious, and each emotional stage irrevocably develops into the next. In the first instant of the prayer: "I put my trust in you, I appeal to you as someone who has power and can be kind; I do not constrain you, I do not attempt to do so—either because I cannot, or will not." (The latter is the more significant example; it marks the final break with the ethics of barbarism.) Secondly, I point out the object of my prayer, its transferable content for which I am asking and which is both real and symbolical. To obtain this transfer is the immediate purpose of my prayer. The third stage is already implicit in the second. I exclaim: "If you will agree to the transfer, that will prove your worth; if you refuse, you will have lowered yourself and I shall be obliged to revise my opinion of you; you will deserve contempt or revenge." Were mine a nobler nature, I would be content to say: "You are the cause of my sadness and responsible for my ruin." But even if the petitioner gives vent to his anger he does not turn to the constraint of a command—unless indeed he abandons the very spirit of

his prayer. A prayer concludes with a judgement, not with an arrest. It makes no promise of paradise regained, but neither is it compatible with robbery under arms.

Prayer is the main instrument by means of which persons come together or drift apart. From its very beginning it proclaims the strengthening or weakening of human bonds; as soon as the petitioner sets it in motion it becomes a test of the participants. "Give me my share of the inheritance; if you don't, you are not really my father; you are neither just nor understanding." Unfortunately, it is to the prodigal himself that these words apply. But whether the father agrees or not, the die is cast; tragedy begins for at least two lives.

(4) Need we go further and speak of the cases where the material content of the prayer coincides with the bond between persons? There are a number of reasons that suggest that we should, and that the steps leading to this ultimate harmony should be defined.

In the first place, the prodigal, having learnt from experience, goes home, and the outcome of the prayer, at the end of much meandering, may, therefore, be successful. The long and painful journey will have led to a mutual understanding. Thinking about it, we have to consider not only what was immediately requested, granted or refused, but also the consequences of deeds done, consequences in embryo in the original request, and perhaps unrealised by the participants or at least by one of them.

However, not all sons are prodigals, nor all fathers misers. Requests and answers exist, dealing indeed with objects distinct from the simple presence of the partners concerned, but which, following a parallel psychological development in each of them, harmoniously reflect the interior symbolism, so that the transition from external to internal reality involves no intrusion of alien elements or any pause or slackening in the interplay of mutual relations.

Lastly, there is the prayer of self-abandonment: a child in its mother's arms, a wife in her husband's embrace. This time no definite petition is made; the choice is left to the other partner. Petition and devotion join together; they may even manage to work the miracle of making a command the tributary of love. "Give me what you command, and command what you will." At any rate, if such a miracle occurs, this is the only way it can occur. Sometimes, in animals, we observe a mysterious hint of this privileged state of trustful abandonment. A sick animal will allow itself to be nursed with disconcerting patience. It is as though it could discern a vet from a butcher! Nevertheless, for an adult human nothing is more repugnant than self-abandonment, and, as a rule, thinking about it does not help matters. A prayer of this kind does not eliminate all objective content, but then neither does it make the object something additional to the persons; it transfigures the object, absorbs it into the total presence of the partners. It is the mutually accepted silence of beings who have achieved perfect inner understanding, so that each asks only for that which the other can give. In fact, they need now ask only for what they have in common or for what constitutes their unity. The thought of the person petitioned forestalls the ideas of the petitioner, or even creates in him the petition he will make. This provides us with the best illustration of what is meant by religious grace. At the highest level of spiritual attainment it is possible for the human intelligence to outstrip another, and promote a development in that other which will nevertheless be an autonomous growth. It is a rare experience, but a decisive one. It gives us an insight into that thing so hard to analyse: the influence exercised by one person on another.

But it would be dangerous to rush to the conclusion that we have already reached this state. All lovers believe that the content of their prayer has completely harmonised the being of the loved one with their own; they think the material world is at their call and joins with them in their enthusiasm; they feel they can carry it off with them, and that through their love they have become so identified with the loved one that he will find nothing foreign to his own nature in the request made to him. "When you grant my petition, are you not granting your own? Are we not co-owners existing in a single being?" The reality, however, is different; love is an ultimate to be achieved, not a starting point. A glimpse is not the journey's end. We have to work for our joy and win it again every day. Community is never so safely established as to be without danger of disintegration, for not one of its members is a stabilised individual. Since each of them is in process of development, the prayer made by each is susceptible of further improvement. Such being the circumstances, the content of a prayer can never be the irrevocable expression of a person's inmost being.

The material content of a prayer is a petition. That was the implied hypothesis we began with, and it is a legitimate one. Is not prayer between man and man always a request? This request, however, can take on strange forms and be wonderfully sublimated. It can become a desire for clearer contemplation, a resolve to be more thoroughly devoted. In love all the elements of prayer are synchronised. Apart from it, although every kind of prayer must contain some traces of contemplation, petition and devotion, these three elements are often separated from one another. They come into existence one after another, not as a unified whole. They are not co-ordinated and are encumbered with incompatible ingredients. Only at the conclusion of an ascending dialectic do they become unified, and in practice we often find ourselves still at the bottom of that ladder.

Is there a material content that belongs in a special way to contemplation and devotion? There certainly is; and it is always some image of the other person and of oneself. But this image is often superficial, fanciful, distorted by partiality. It necessarily creates a relationship between I and Thou, and yet false attitudes so often intervene. Even self-offering may be foolish and sinful. This help I am striving to give you, this service I claim to be doing you, may, in fact, be ludicrous and degrading. Only in the search for the genuine and authentic self is salvation to be found. When prayer eliminates the non-I and the non-Thou, it transforms its contents and crosses the frontier into another world in which it still has content and vitality, but no longer estranges us from essential reality.

2. *The Formal Content*

The formal content is the way in which the material elements are conjoined. And since in all prayer, whether noble or vile, petition is the outstanding feature, its formal content will normally be that of a plea.

Why should one plead? Because there is some deficiency in the other person's observation. The petitioner cannot nakedly expose his needs. He must, therefore, speak in such a way as to make clear the situation, real or imaginary. He will inform the other person of the extent and nature of what he lacks: "I am just out of hospital, I've just been discharged from prison, I need money for food while I'm looking for a job; I need £5 for the train-fare home. You did not know, but I am telling you. Help me!" To this disclosure of the situation another is added: "You must get to know all about me, who I am, what I am. Here is my identity card and certificate of good conduct; I am a respectable chap, or, if I have not always been so, at least believe that I can be redeemed. This may not be written on my face, but it is engraved in my plea. Allow me to be your informant, and the advocate of my own cause."

A plea is usually an *apologia pro vita sua*. But it is not necessarily so. In the first place there are, though infrequently, humble prayers in which a man is willing to admit to a fellow man the wrong he has done: "I do not deserve it, but, in spite of that, give me a helping hand." The petitioner, contrite and humbled though he is, still presents himself as worthy of trust *qua* petitioner; it is one of the laws of prayer that the consciousness of the person praying is on a level loftier than that of his existence when he is not praying. Then, there are pleas for others: intercessions, recommendations, persuasions. Andromache's plea was mainly of this type; with perfect harmony it sums up every aspect since it includes her own personal request: "Hector, have compassion on your son, yourself and your wife." Lastly, there are pleas for a collective cause, or for some impersonal good: "Think of your country; do not allow its art collections and laboratories to be destroyed; safeguard the rights of the mind, etc." In such appeals deceit remains a possibility, but it no longer has any natural relationship with them. In principle and often in fact they confront us with the noblest impulses that move human hearts towards one another. In the highest instances, men meet and assist one another for a divine cause only, and no longer for their own sakes or for their earthly interests.

This change in material content has repercussions on the form.

We have advanced from egocentric apologia to the defence of another's case, and finally to the presentation of some intrinsic value. Nevertheless the fundamental character of the form is unchangeable; it is always a persuasive appeal doing its best to be objective. These last words raise a disturbing problem, for prayer can never rid itself of a duality in its form: it is both an allurement and a kind of reasoning. But what part can reasoning have in allurement? Petition in its aspect of begging is primarily emotional, in its noble forms it is primarily objective; but from its base to its summit it includes, in varying proportions, a strategy of the feelings as well as a chain of reasoning. It wants to charm and also to convince. Ought it not to choose, if it would be honest? Will it use the intellect in order to delude the heart? Or is the emotional element in it only provisional, finding its fulfilment in the logic of an impersonal utterance?

In order to answer this question and to appreciate the fact that in prayer emotion is not meant to remain irrational, nor reason to keep apart from the subjective realm, it will be useful to distinguish two contrasted cases: prayer that is insincere and prayer that is genuine.

(1) Consider the first case. Prayer of this kind is made with intent to deceive. It is attempted deceit if I try to dupe the other person with regard to my real motives. In spite of appearances, in such deceit I show more respect for the other person than I do for myself, for, aiming at what is best in him, I have to do much thinking in order to try and give consistency to those images of myself which I either distort or invent. But prayer can also be attempted corruption. In that case it is in fact temptation, and every temptation is a prayer. He who tempts another is not only false to himself; he is false also to his partner whose weak spot he tries to find and whose complicity he seeks to secure. "I deliberately intend not only to deceive you about my position and myself, but I also mean to deceive both myself and you about your position and yourself. I want us both to yield to the excitement of being accomplices and both to agree in a falsehood." If we did not know it to be a falsehood, the prayer would be less culpable and less attractive, and since

such ignorance differs in degree in each of the partners, the perversity of one of them can consciously destroy the innocence of the other. There is, indeed, bound to be this gap to be bridged, because it is a question of prayer and, therefore, of resistance to be overcome. But though the corruption of the innocent may require effort, the resistance put up by the already corrupt is an encouraging artifice that quickly succumbs to the tempter. The latter will speak with gestures, looks and silent invitation; he will have no need to argue because agreement has already been reached on the secondary principles of the action, whereas, in the case of deceiving an honest partner, there would only be agreement on the first principles of the process of reasoning.

From this demonstration it is easy to see that the destinies of both feeling and idea leave the right path together in an insincere prayer, and especially in temptation. There is not the least incompatibility between allurement and intellection; on the contrary, allurement is a way of understanding and then of lying by hiding what one continues to understand. According to circumstances, the deviation will either be unilateral, or agreed upon by the two persons concerned. But should the tempter meet with a refusal, he can often do without the formal apparatus of reasoning, for even in the holiest of men a menagerie of monsters exists quite able to ensure that the tempter shall be understood before being rejected. Fake maxims (it doesn't pay to be honest, the pleasures of vice are exquisite, etc.) spring up and act as persuaders for the acceptance of the material thing offered; a cheque held out or a caress insinuated, contain an implicit philosophy that deceives no one. The abstract theory of a sophist, on the other hand, is nearer to deceit than to temptation for its material consequences are not always apparent, and this is why unwholesome thinkers argue more than bandits and are more boring. It takes them years to learn how to tempt themselves and to let loose the animal from the swaddling-clothes in which the idea of it had been buried. But, there is no separating the pathology of the emotions from that of the intelligence.

Flattery of good feelings may assist the efforts of deception, and flattery of evil feelings those of temptation. But this will not alter the relationship between the factors concerned. Always there will be a deviation of the emotions and the mind together; the only difference is that by flattery one tries, if one is a tempter, to superimpose deceit upon temptation, and when one is a deceiver, to superimpose temptation upon deceit. But the basic analysis keeps its truth unaltered: both temptation and deceit have this in common—they involve their authors in a lie that is addressed simultaneously to the emotions and the mind. In deception, the liar does not utter his lie in order that it may be infectious, but in order that it may be profitable; hence the façade of impeccable logic he offers, with the aim of substituting a series of imaginary elements carefully co-ordinated in a logical sequence, for the dubious characteristics of his real nature. The tempter's plea, on the other hand, aims at planting the lie in his partner's heart, where it may become the settled assumption of emotions and a mind that clothe their real values in a guise of one-sided or fictitious appearance.

(2) We will scrutinise now the prayer that is sincere, i.e. that keeps faithful to the truth. The conduct just described is reversed; sophisms of head and heart disappear. And the parallel course of persuasion and objectivity becomes even more obvious. Occasionally, no doubt, in the development of the objective aspect of a prayer, a set of words may be included that could be separated from it. An example of this can be found in the accounts of warlike deeds and in the historical passages which Xenophon inserts in his speeches to his soldiers. These enable him to conclude: "Follow me, you can see how right I was, and that I did everything possible for your safety." Still, however objective the content and the mode of the plea may be, it is bound to be related to the persons concerned. The ideas it contains are not systems wandering on their own; they are always connected with the persons involved in the prayer. This latter views everything *sub specie personarum*. If it did not do so, there would be no question of obtaining anything from the other person, or of offering him anything. We must, therefore, modify what we said above with regard to impersonal petitions: even in the work for a divine and impersonal cause an aspect of I and Thou is really present; the moment prayer between two persons begins, this

element awakes and struggles for recognition. All impersonal values become humanised and individualised as soon as I strive to make them loved; they come into the story of one person's development. Indeed their involvement in that story is so deep that the pure logic of ideas cannot assume and absorb the persuasive appeal; on the contrary, it serves it.

Does this mean that the formal content of prayer belongs to rhetoric and not to logic? If we leave sophism on one side, then the rhetoric that remains deserves all the attention and the praise assigned to it, for example, by C. Perelman. It follows that very often "we must be content with what is plausible and that our judgements seldom succeed in reaching what is necessary". The determination of the degrees of probability or of the ways in which these may be made obvious to others, deserves a study on its own.[2] Is not prayer, in this sense, always a plea, and must it not be entirely a manifestation of rhetoric?

This is no doubt true. And yet two aspects of its form require to be distinguished. If we want to plead a cause that would seem, at first sight, altogether impersonal, e.g. the needs of the blind or, *a fortiori*, the drawing up of a geological map of the Sahara, there is no obvious reason why a barrister should set about the task differently from a scientist. Prayer begins, however, when the scientist admits that there is no reality that is not a matter of human concern, and when he makes himself an advocate of this human concern. At that moment, rhetoric also begins. Public opinion must be aroused, what seems impersonal must be subjected to an interpersonal undertaking, an undertaking which is in fact our own destiny. The facts about the blind or about the geology of the Sahara suddenly acquire a new coefficient of urgency and become a part of the problem of our own existence. And since we continue to grope about until we die, since we are always trying to become what we really are, and our deeds are never more than partly born, we shall never be in the

[2] C. Perelman and Olbrechts-Tyteca, *Traité de l'argumentation*, Paris, 1958, 2 vols., *passim*. I disagree, however, with Perelman when he seems to affirm that only sociological grounds can provide criteria for relative truth; and also when he appears to dissociate the intellectual and affective elements in persuasion. To me their osmosis seems inescapable.

position where there is no need to pray. Our prayers form part of that incessant becoming in which human beings call to each other and influence each other so that they may reach their destination. Such rhetoric should not be considered lower than logic or alien to it; in fact it *is* the logic of acts of communication. Like logic of every kind, it contains the law of non-contradiction and universality. But it cannot be static, for it deals with beings who, not having ceased to live, cannot cease to try to elucidate the theme of their being from amidst the variations of their life history.

Lastly, we come to the final and most important reason why prayer moves in a single movement towards objectivity and allurement. It is an appeal to another man's heart. The individual who makes it realises that he is not equal to his task, if he remains alone. Underlying the discussion or argument (when it is not hypocritical) is a confession of inadequacy and a mutual appeal. Prayer is this confession in its initial stage, before the dialogue has been infected by vanity or the will to dominate. It is a plea, but with the consciousness that there is something lacking in my plea. What is lacking is not only the satisfaction of my desire to possess; at a much deeper level it is the acquisition of an authentic—and absolute—value. The very fact of my being moved to pray makes me realise my own inadequacy, and that includes the inadequacy of my prayer and of the reasons it adduces. The request and the offering I put forward, the contemplation I seek—all converges on the same conviction: "I have no absolute certainty, and your wider knowledge can help me. The freedom you enjoy contains some illumination for my mind; do not keep it from me!" Thus, even on the human level, prayer implies a philosophy open to development: through prayer I come to realise that my *logos* is *eikon* and that my reason is as yet germinal. In order that it may grow and ramify into a system of forms adequate to their content, this seed of reason needs more space than it can find within my isolated self. There is, therefore, a mutual immanence of reason and personality both in the "I" and beyond it, and it is this that explains the osmosis of persuasion and objectivity and also the fact that its perfection is promissory only.

CHAPTER 3

The Man Who Makes the Prayer

Prayer between human beings must be examined first of all as it exists in the person who prays. This discloses the structure of prayer, and especially the ground in which it is rooted, the subjective conditions it presupposes.

It would be too simple to say that prayer is a woman's affair, whilst to command pertains to man. In the language of characterology, an inclination to implore is indicative of the Venus type, and an inclination to issue orders shows that the type is Mars. But the theorists of this brand of psychology agree that these types are not rigidly confined to different sexes. Nothing very valuable emerges from an insistence on the femininity of the prayerful character. Males will beg when they feel the need. De Vigny's wolf is fictitious, because wolves live in a pack; when they are alone and hungry, they beg for food, like other animals.[1]

It would be equally stupid to limit prayer to any particular time of life. Hesiod said: "Work for youth; deliberation for maturity; prayer for the aged."[2] But what does a baby do except call for attention from his parents or his nurse? The truth is that the connexion between need and prayer is very much closer than that between prayer and age or sex.

1. Prayer is an Avowal of Inadequacy

This avowal is self-evident if my prayer consists in a request for material service or money. There are two variants here. Either I am genuinely impoverished and unable to obtain what I want by my

---

[1][The reference is to Alfred de Vigny's famous poem: *La Mort du loup*, where we read, for example: *Gémir, pleurer, prier est également lâche.—Translator.*]

[2] Ἔργα νέων, βουλαὶ δὲ μέσων, εὐχαὶ δὲ γερόντων, Hesiod, *Fragment* 65.

own efforts; or else I could obtain it, but through laziness or selfishness, I would rather have it supplied for me. In either case, I consider that what I lack can be given me by another. The only difference is that in the second case what I lack is not so much material
wealth as the courage to secure it by my own activity. I ask someone
else to give me what I want by adding a measure of deception to my
prayer, or by playing upon a weakness in him, in the way described
above. Whether honourable or not, the limitations imposed upon
the self when it is isolated reveal themselves in petition and that is
why it is humiliating. If the limitations are culpable, then the
humiliation is less obvious, but more profound.

Prayers might be classified according to the limitations they admit.
These may clearly be more or less substantial: "Please pass the
jam", and: "Throw me a life-belt. I'm drowning!" are not on the
same level of seriousness. Some requests carry no urgency or direct
appeal: others are an SOS to the only person who can help.

Petitions may spring from a natural or an artificial need. A
cobbler's needs are more natural than a financier's. But whatever its
origin, a petition indicates that the person who makes it cannot
maintain himself within his own territory. This is particularly true
of infants who before they can speak are able to cry and make a
noise, i.e. to demand from society that part of their individuality
which they do not yet possess. An adult, on the other hand, may
play the part of Robinson Crusoe, withdraw to his ivory tower and
live in solitude on the capital he has acquired from petitions previously granted. From the point of view of moral values, old age
should be the period when these are least lacking, but physically it is
a return to the weakness and dependence of infancy.

This avowal of limitation can be observed not only in the prayer
of petition, but also in contemplation. A mother who looks at her
child, a friend who seeks the companionship of his friend, are both
in need of a presence. They admit that they cannot live without it;
in its absence they feel incomplete. This is, in fact, the proof that
prayer always includes petition, at least the request that the other
person should allow me to look on him and should not reject the
mutual sympathy which I long for between his being and my own.

The prayer of contemplation is more necessary to the petitioner than the other requests; it is the contact which, once it is established, makes these further steps possible. Of course, the self-seeking petition moves on at once from the original contact, but the most abject beggar cannot help starting from what amounts to an act of contemplation: he has to take a look at the other person before he attempts to get hold of his possessions or to benefit from his activity. If we now quit such squalid aberrations and, dismissing material demands, rise to the simple contemplation of another person, we shall remain faithful to the law of personal growth, which can never be anything but a development in dependence upon the relation between one person and another. Prayer, therefore, is, even philosophically, important, for it is prayer that makes plain the interrelatedness of men and the fact that a man only becomes human among his brethren. This remark has as its corollary that the injury and mutilation of the self sustained by a misanthrope, or—but in a different way—by a husband deserted by his wife, are graver than would be the case for some wretch dying of hunger in a wilderness.

Would it not be more dignified never to ask anyone for anything? There is indeed a sense in which independence is the ideal for the self in its relation to men and nature. But ultimately this is a delusion; the transitory nature of our existence constantly denies it. Diogenes may personally have dispensed with other people, and yet there is something missing in his greatness because of his not asking others to help their neighbours, because of his not "praying" for the success of the cynic philosophy he professed. Of course, in the last resort, his life was a prayer and his behaviour a sermon. On the other hand, it may be said that he lacked devotion and that, as a sage, he was a mutilated one. Even intellectually he missed that breadth of vision which a sense of dependence would have given him. It would seem, therefore, that without going so far as to reproach him with replacing cowardice with pride, there are many reasons for asserting that prayer between human beings in no way dwarfs a man. The act of praying is not a sign of cowardice, although the mode of praying may be.

2. Prayer is the Expression of Dominant Desire

On this point an American author has written: "Prayer, in this more inclusive sense, is the settled craving of a man's heart, *good or bad*, his inward love and determining desire.... In this sense, Columbus' search for America was prayer; Edison's long attempt to find the secret of incandescence was prayer; Paul's ambition to found Christian churches and Napoleon's ambition to rule Europe both were prayers.... Any man who after money or fame or pleasure insistently directs his course, has in his dominant desire the prayer that shapes his life."[3]

This is a remarkable paragraph, but it exaggerates. A dominant desire does not, of itself, constitute a prayer; for that desire to become a prayer a personal appeal is necessary. A desire for impersonal objects such as money or glory cannot rightly be equated with authentic prayer, for the good reason that prayer presupposes a listener, or at least someone who hears. We might, of course, assert that our dominant desires presuppose hidden listeners, and that, in fact, we are for ever on the look-out for a meeting with the whole range of beings. Looked at in this way, human life would be a perpetual call, directed to visible or invisible intelligences, and ultimately to God; we should exist in a latent and uninterrupted state of prayer. The problem then would not be whether we ought to pray, but how we should do so correctly.

But this, too, would seem to be an exaggeration, for we often shut ourselves off from the presence of others and our intellectual life itself can work in two directions: it may either organise reality, fencing itself all round in the process, or it may open itself up to the incomprehensible. With regard to the world of nature, we do not pray to its phenomena; we either put up with them or we foresee them and hold ourselves in readiness. Only towards the animal world can we be said sometimes to be in a relation of mutual living intercourse, and this relationship is not identical with the dialogue between human beings.[4] The realisation that we are surrounded by

[3] H. E. Fosdick, *The Meaning of Prayer*, VIII. First published 1915, Fontana, 1962, pp. 166–7.
[4] A physicist in his experiments puts material things upon the rack: he asks

other beings does not *ipso facto* begin a conversation, and although prayer may be the expression of a person's dominant desire, that desire alone is not prayer.

An additional remark on this point is imperative: the dominant desire of one moment is itself dominated at another moment. On different days we demand different and contradictory things from our surroundings. Sometimes our personality is so ill organised that no one element predominates. Even if one element does predominate, it can either arise spontaneously or be the result of reflexion or of a decision of the will. We labour to develop a dominant desire, we submit to it; we build our personality by means of it. This means some one element in us controls the rest. The Cid or Polyeucte ponder the issues at stake; the attitudes they envisage sway now this way, now that, until they arrive at a definite choice. The point may perhaps be better expressed by saying that prayer is an indication either of a desire that is struggling to the surface, or of one that is already in control. The two are rarely found to be in immediate agreement, and prayer often provides evidence of a transitional situation or of an inner conflict. That is why its development and its apparent lack of systematic coherence are so instructive. A person who prays is trying to give a logical form to what he is saying, but the course of these attempts is not always logical.

3. *In Prayer a Man Discovers what he Wants*

This idea both corrects and completes the previous paragraph. Quite often we do not know exactly what we want; we ask, we offer, vehemently, and yet do not really know what we are asking for or offering, or to whom we are speaking. There is an effervescence which precedes prayer and proclaims its approach. St Augustine expresses this in the Third Book of his *Confessions*: "I sought some object for my love; I was in love with love. I hated the idea of

questions and obtains answers, but the ensuing "dialogue" has nothing in common with that between two minds. The poet's intercourse with nature is closer to a relationship between persons, but this is obviously outside the limits of our present discussion.

comfort, of a life without snares."[5] So, youth's quest in the world
is inspired by a spirit of adventure, unrestricted by any particular
object; a young man has no idea where the treachery or the advantages of experience may land him. In modern terminology, he is
unconscious of the dialectic of his deeds.

In the examples taken from Homer in the last chapter, it is true
that Andromache and Priam showed no hesitation; they knew at
once what they were aiming at. (It was Hector and Achilles who
were uncertain; Achilles, at least, was, since he permitted his mind
to be changed.) And yet Andromache and Priam by expressing what
they wanted and by hearing the response they obtained, gave direction to their conduct and confirmed or altered what they meant to
do. So even in their case, they learnt what they really wanted through
the act of expressing it. They acquired a clearer vision of what remained to be done.

In many other cases, even among Homer's heroes and gods,
prayer is less straightforward in its effect. A parallel development is
discernible in its various elements. The man who prays, the recipient of his prayer, the prayer itself—all interact and collaborate in the
production of something definite. The really activating factor may,
of course, vary. Sometimes it is the meeting with my friend that
makes me aware of what I would ask from him, and helps me to
become what I ought to be. Sometimes it is through becoming personally more mature that I learn what friendship means; or, finally,
it may be that through expressing friendship I come to realise both
what I need and the one who can satisfy that need. Quite often the
mere fact of having to set out a request in an explicit form necessitates either its clear definition or else some modification of it. It may
even happen that the attempt to express a request results either in
asking for its opposite or for nothing at all. This is a comic or tragic
consequence frequently utilised by dramatists. In Molière's *Don
Juan*, for example, M. Dimanche is trying to get repayment from
Don Juan of some money owed to him, but he comes back empty-
handed: "He was so overpoweringly polite and complimentary that

[5] *Confessions*, 3, 1, 1.

it would have been out of the question to ask him for money." The unfortunate M. Dimanche could not get a word in edgeways to state his claim; he was swamped by his creditor's oratory. It would have been better if he had stayed at home and employed a debt-collector!

CHAPTER 4

The Man Who Receives the Prayer

If no one was present, I should not ask anything from anyone. But what is meant by presence? This is an initial problem and a formidable one. Next in order is the problem of response, and this normally presupposes an element of freedom on the part of my partner.

1. *The Presence of the Recipient of Prayer*

(1) A beggar is following me; either he saw me, or I was pointed out to him. In some shape or other I have become something on his horizon. The mere fact that I exist in this world is defined, as far as I am concerned, by the possibility of my being observed by all those who make up the world, and the certainty that some of them will observe me. What precisely is the core of reality that emanates from the personality? What is the basic fact of this datum? Is it simply a material entity? It cannot be only that, for dead bodies and not their spirits which are presumed to survive them would then be the object of our prayers. We must call it a material entity quickened by life. Is that enough? Others perceive in my living body something which seems capable of being incorporated in the development of their own lives and of relating me to their major interests. To the beggar I am seen as a possible donor, first- or second-class, or as a non-donor. In any case I am classified. This idea of me is really a conclusion drawn by the beggar from some of my gestures he has observed and also from a calculation of the extent of his influence or non-influence over me. Sometimes this calculation is very precise, e.g. is the probable amount of the alms I shall give worth all the bother involved in hurrying to catch up with me?

However, to the extent to which prayer is not merely a means to a material end, but involves a direct appeal to an individual, we have to admit that my presence appears first of all as a unique and irreplaceable invitation. It is not so much what I do that attracts, but my way of doing it. An individual may wear a mask, he may be mistaken for someone else, and yet what is original in him will still break through. There must be something ultimate perceptible from the start, or a person would never be known or able to be known. From the very beginning, what prevents any rupture between appearance and reality in the perception of me as a person is a certain feeling, at least, of the final achievement.

Of course, the actual perception made of me will vary in depth and disinterestedness according to the individuals who do the perceiving. This is due not only to the fact that observers' intelligences can vary in the acuity of their perception, but also to the further fact that such perception is affected by a variety of factors: circumstances may act as a distorting screen; self-interest and cupidity may interpose an image between me and the man observing me, an image which is his creation, not mine. What is more, even my physical appearance can be a screen rather than a filter. According to Porphyry, Plotinus would not allow his portrait to be painted because he thought that even the living face was impotent to express and transmit the inner self. This is an extreme point of view, but it is true that appearance does in some degree conceal what is really present. There are degrees of contact in our meetings.

When, however, a meeting does take place, the beam that reaches you illuminates me also. Our perception of other people fundamentally implies an awareness of ourselves as well as of them. The relevant metaphor is that of the crossroads. If, on the other hand, we deny that duality is involved in such intuition we cease to be able to affirm even the *cogito* of the personal thinking subject, and then to vindicate the existence of others who are related to it. Even so, it still remains true that this is an intuition of an I and a Thou which are very imperfect and incomplete. They are simply recognised as an essentially original way of being summoned to personal development and completion. Their outlines glimpsed in the first perception will tend towards an ever closer definition as the series of perceptions is prolonged.

(2) The beggar would not follow me unless he cherished the hope of catching up with me, i.e. of being himself observed in a relationship of I and Thou analogous to that between myself and him which his pursuit implies. The new relationship would run parallel with the old. He believes he might make his presence felt, or, to express it differently, that I might discover him.

When a man (and especially a beggar) "prays", he is beginning a real battle to get himself noticed. Physical and social obstacles that prevent recognition have to be overcome. He has to plant himself in some place where a meeting is inevitable, and when he has found that place he must ascertain the exact moment that will secure attention. Then, when he has actually been perceived by me, when the two circuits of perception (I–Thou from the beggar's end, and I–Thou from the donor's end) have been established, have we at least reached the perfect prayer? Not at all! Even if the relationship is not one of begging, but of friendship or love, the struggle turns inward and becomes fiercer; a chasm opens up before the two concerned. They may have been intimately related in the past, their present prayer may be very eloquent, but each of them knows that their existences do not coincide, and will never form a seamless robe. If we return to the metaphor of the crossroads, then each road vanishes ahead and behind in that stretch of space that is proper to each alone. The two persons who are present to each other are also absent from each other; their life-lines do not run parallel and cannot be mutually influential in every respect. Earlier on we spoke of a twofold datum; now we have to discuss a reciprocal transcendence. This too is a matter of degree; sometimes, after the manner of those eighteenth-century portraits that have caught a living instant and reveal the soul in the outlines of the flesh, the communion that results from sight is instantaneous; sometimes it seems to cover a long period of the past or present and suggests an unlimited future. In that case my perception of you admits the mystery in you, and admits its stability. And yet even this stability may be a delusion; our immediate awareness of it is not probative, nor is the personal presence really reassuring. The transcendency of being is elusive and difficult to pin down; it does not declare itself wholly as transcendency in a moment of brief contact, and it does not develop into the intimacy of perfect symbiosis which would destroy it. Our personalities are always developing and never complete; therefore they cannot explain themselves to one another by that sort of influence which would really be nothing short of total and absolute creation *ex nihilo*. It is, therefore, a substantial achievement to have made sure that one is perceived by another person, and yet this is only the initial move towards mutual awareness, and prayer cannot be satisfied with that.

(3) What then comes next? Having perceived this other person, having in turn been perceived by him, I now appeal to him, and this direct approach marks an advance on the impact made at the start by our mutual presence. I may be intensely aware that there is some being at my side and yet make no move towards him. This in fact is our attitude to *things* and to persons considered as things. But when I make a personal appeal to someone, I move on to a different plane. It is an experience which is at the heart of every prayer and which cannot be deduced or explained. The vocative case is not deduced from the nominative; it is the reverse process which is normal.[1] The awareness of presence has now come to include a decision to break the silence and to have it broken by the other's response; the inner struggle is now carried on with a fresh achievement in view: my aim now is not to get my presence recognised, for that has been done; it is to secure recognition for the worth of my prayer. Using to their utmost my powers of persuasion, I am out to convince. Does this mean that I may legitimately try to force the decision of him to whom I am appealing? It does not; for that would be to exceed the limits and norms of prayer, which is

[1] This priority of the *thou* over the *he* and its power to bring the *he* into being are seldom admitted in philosophy: Coleridge, Martin Buber and perhaps Gabriel Marcel have sketched the theory (cf. on Marcel, R. Troisfontaines, *De l'Existence à l'être*, Louvain & Paris, 1954, vol. 2, pp. 27 ff.). See also with regard to the origin of the idea of truth, the summary of J. MacMurray's thought in J. Pucelle, *La Source des valeurs*, Paris, 1957, pp. 155–6. On the other hand, the derivation of the ideas of number, substance, etc., from the idea of the self has frequently been attempted, especially by Descartes and Fichte.

not a command, and which awaits in fear and trembling the unfore-seeable response that the other person will make. Even when it has succeeded in its work of persuasion, prayer has not yet been granted a decision; in fact, so long as it remains authentically prayer, decision remains outside its sphere. This is why the awareness of presence in prayer remains, especially before it is answered, or apart from a favourable answer, an awareness of transcendence. This is the threshold at which the closer and closer approaches and the considerable ingredient of activity involved in the complex reality of presence, must inevitably pause.

It is this complexity that makes so wretchedly inadequate the psychological theories that have been built up in order to account for this awareness of presence. When Ribot would have us consider the physiological conditions, when James has recourse to the irrup-tion of the unconscious, they do not really explain this awareness and they sidestep the problem of appeal. For the same reasons, it would be quite inadequate to define presence as the mobilisation of energies or as the transformation effected in the self. For such effects could equally well be produced by an impersonal idea. But when the issue is that of another person's presence, then the fact is that what is aimed at is something quite different, and this fact cannot be explained in terms of anything else. It is true, of course, that if I am aware of another's presence, that awareness may agitate me, but the agitation is not a sufficient description of the presence, and still less of the appeal, unless these two realities are surreptitiously introduced.

An example may illustrate this analytical procedure. Consider the case of a very sick man who cannot do without the person who looks after him. What are the elements involved in the situation? First of all there is the meeting, now become habitual, between the sick man and his nurse: this is the first stage noted above, that of the mutual perception and of the minimum of influence which the situation makes inevitable.

Then follows the prayer which will aim at making the presence a lasting one, inducing it to become active in some definite way, even at the risk of provoking a crisis: "I beg you not to leave me, not to go away. I want you, you alone, to look after me." This might be called the outgoing influence involved in prayer even when it is mainly contemplative (what I need supremely is that you will stay by my side, and that I may see you; that is why I want no one else; I refuse to go into hospital; the simple fact of your presence is all the assistance I need on my death-bed).

In declarations like these we see that there is self-disclosure (I am sick, I need you, such is my emotional state, etc.). But they also indicate a stratagem. For in order to disclose to you what I am and what I need, I have to stress one point of view, and the action I take is a reflexion of the development of my character: I have to make a choice from among its possibilities and offer you one of its aspects to the exclusion of others. Hence the temptation for me to dissemble and to play on your compassion or to exaggerate my sickness. I may perhaps try to invade the sphere of your transcendence and appeal to "sacred" motives that will compel you to agree (*obsecratio*): in the name of God, in the name of your children, remain at my bedside. This is undoubtedly the element which disturbs the integrity of prayer; it is an assault on the bastion of the other's freedom, and a desperate effort to extract the hoped-for decision. Hence the promises and praises, sometimes merely implied, that accompany it (you will be able to say that you were the one to whom I was most attached in my last illness, the one I called for right to the end, the one who best cared for me for my own sake, etc.). This kind of thing on a lower level becomes a suggested bargain (stay, and I will leave you my fortune).

This prayer which oversteps the mark also becomes strangely detached from the self and attempts all kinds of trickery; it lies and at the same time tries to force the issue. The self does, of course, throw itself into the request with the impetuosity of despair, but it makes use of exaggerations or falsehoods, without scruple. The most moving form of prayer, on the other hand, is the least obtrusive, that which discloses the self as it really is, without trappings and in all its distress. It ceases to be calculating and becomes self-abandonment to another. It tends, moreover, to be silent and filled with awe. Speech is put aside because it can only express the truth partially and approximately, whereas I am seeking all things by giving all things. The motive of the prayer is no longer distinct from the person praying. Whilst being a request it is also a burnt-offering. "Do with me what seems good to you. My fate is in your hands. I trust you." Selfless prayer is pure love, without any shadow of a threat, or of resentment in case of refusal (even though this latter cannot be thought of without despair). It leaves the initiative for a concrete reply to the other person; it suggests nothing at all, because it realises that the other already knows all the suggestions, and it wants to secure for him the freedom of utter impartiality; above all things it wants him to be free.

The urgency of the situation, however, and the mediocrity of both petitioner and recipient make it rare that the relationship between minds and hearts is of such an exalted quality. Before any conjunction of soul, presence presupposes a material struggle to secure the perception of the self and the acceptance of the well-grounded nature of its desires. But presence of the most intimate kind goes further than this preamble; it consists in a meeting between two free beings who salute each other, even though with drawn swords, and, more than this, a convergence of their wills and of the love which unites them. It is for this reason that presence becomes a lower thing when the petitioner ceases to respect the autonomy of the person to whom he is appealing and only regards him as an instrument.

2. The Recipient's Answer

Fully to believe in another's presence is, therefore, to believe in his freedom. This belief *ipso facto* admits the possibility of a reply that may add something of its own to our prayers even when it grants what they had asked for and appears, moreover, to follow on their having been made. It also implies belief in a return influence of the Thou on the I, just as petition presupposed belief in an outgoing influence on the petitioner. We will now examine this notion of response and briefly describe its forms and structure.

In its elementary stage, a reply is free of any kind of counter-request; indeed it is the cancellation of the initial request by the one who replies to it. This cancellation is shown in three main ways: acceptance, refusal or evasion.

Each of these three attitudes is worth an extended study. The classical masterpieces to which we have so often referred provide ample material for analysis and reflexion on this matter. For example, how much light is thrown on the development and outcome of supplication by the *Odyssey*.

In Book 22, during the slaughter of the suitors, the episode of Leodes contains a remarkable and grim refusal:

> Leodes rushed forward and clasped Odysseus' knees and burst into an anguished appeal: "I throw myself on your mercy, Odysseus. Have some regard and pity for me. I swear to you that never by word or deed have I done wrong to a woman in the house. In fact I did my best to hold them all back from such evil courses. But they wouldn't listen when I told them to keep their hands from mischief, and their own iniquities have brought them to this awful pass. But I was only their priest; I did nothing. And now I am to share their fate! That is all the thanks one gets for the goodness one has shown."
>
> Odysseus looked at him with disgust. "You say you were their priest," he answered. "How often, then, you must have prayed in this hall that the happy day of my return might be put off, and that my dear wife might be yours and bear your children. For that, nothing shall save you from the bitterness of death."[2]

A little further on, the minstrel Phemius also appeals to Ulysses, and warns him that he will repent later if he kills a minstrel like himself, who sings for gods and men. He asserts that he had sung at the suitors' banquets only when brute force and numbers dragged him there. All this would probably not have saved his life had Telemachus not interceded in turn for the unfortunate poet and borne witness to his innocence. Ulysses allows himself to be convinced and answers, smiling: "Dismiss your fears. My son has saved you from the jaws of death to teach you the lesson, which I hope you'll take to heart and preach, that virtue is a better policy than vice."[3] This is an example of acceptance, but the prayer was not heard

---

[2] *Odyssey*, 22, 310–25. [Trans. E. V. Rieu, Penguin Classics, p. 346.]
[3] Ibid., 330–77. [Rieu, p. 348.]

without Telemachus' assistance, nor was it in precisely the sense and for the motives which Phemius had proposed.[4]

Lastly, Penelope provides us, in Book 23, with an example of an evasive reply. She conceals her mistrust under an agreement in principle; let the bed be prepared for the stranger so that he may rest, as he has asked. But in reality Penelope was testing Ulysses by letting him know that his bed had been moved outside the nuptial chamber:

> "You too are strange," said the cautious Penelope. "I am not being haughty or indifferent. I am not even unduly surprised. But I have too clear a picture of you in my mind when you sailed from Ithaca in your long-oared ship. Come, Eurycleia, make him a comfortable bed outside the bedroom that he built so well himself. Place the big bed out there, and make it up with rugs and blankets, and with laundered sheets."[5]

In this case, the answer by evasion was a kind of trap or counter-question. It thus comes close to what it sometimes really is: the working out of a synthesis of behaviour which transcends both acceptance and refusal. But much more often it is merely a prosaic compromise.

Acceptance, refusal and evasion are what seem to be the different modes of reply. But a closer look reveals that the reality of a reply does not necessarily correspond with its appearance. For example, a persistent pursuit may be diverted by a present. A superficial acceptance of the request may sometimes mean that it has inwardly been rejected, whereas a superficial rejection may conceal the fact that it has been inwardly granted. Knowing when to say No can

[4] These stages are even more precise in Racine's *Britannicus*: Agrippine appeals to Nero in vain, although making some impression on him; then Burrhus pleads for Britannicus' pardon and obtains it. But this success through accumulated effort is later compromised by Narcisse, and we come back to a refusal which we immediately feel will now be more pitiless than the criminal's original intention.

In *Bérénice*, the end of Act V and the climax of the whole tragedy result from a similar accumulation. What Titus' heroic prayer cannot obtain from Bérénice, the heroic prayer by Antiochus (by whom she is loved, but whom she does not love) finally does procure. Prayer which is also an example becomes almost irresistible.

[5] *Odyssey*, 23, 174–80. [Rieu, p. 356.]

sometimes be the secret of a good educationist. In teaching, denial and shock-treatment have a mysterious part to play. "Your homework is an absolute disgrace! Do it all again! You want to learn, do you? Very well then, I am granting your deepest wish by preventing you from fulfilling the desires that are not worthy of you." With regard to the reply by evasion, on the other hand (a reply that may be for the best or the worst), it favours the resumption of the dialogue, and if that happens, then the reply really amounts to a counter-proposal. The whole process starts all over again in a new form.

At the very highest stage of the relationship between persons, the reply inevitably becomes both an offering and a request in its turn: it involves the exchange of mutual vows of friendship and love. It is the condition in which one ceases to request anything for oneself because one is giving oneself and in that sense it is allowable to ask for all things. We shall then have rejoined, but on a higher level and with both partners fully active, what had begun by being a joint awareness and perception and has now been enriched by the contribution of two decisions in harmony.

The return influence thus completes, in one of several possible ways, the cycle begun by the joint influence of the initial perceptions and, later, by the outgoing influence of the request. The crisis has been resolved. The reply has brought the hope to a happy or unhappy conclusion. It has done away with the precise objective of the prayer by giving it a refusal, an acceptance, or a transformation. The initial outgoing influence of the request was restricted to suggestion only; the return influence of the response works like a mighty force. Should the reply be a refusal, this force in no way continues the movement begun by the request; if it is a real refusal it separates the two partners and destroys their co-presence, or, in any case, gives it a new and pathetic form: when Aeneas had left her, what remained of him for Dido, except a nagging, intolerable and dangerous memory? And how much of Dido's presence remained for Aeneas?

But when the influence is that of a petition that has been granted, it establishes and confirms a spiritual communion; from consent there springs an irresistible grace. The influence of the initial request resembled what in theology would be called a "sufficient grace", which is not necessarily accompanied by "efficacious grace". But the disparity between the return influence and the outgoing one disappears on the heights and a joint influence is produced, originating in free decision inspired by love.

3. *The Parts Played by Reason and Freedom in the Reply*

Between the question and its answer, the personality of the other man is inserted actively and unpredictably. I may perhaps corner him, or at least put him to the test (the most subtle way of testing is the discreet approach: "I don't want to be a dun, but . . ."). But although I may foresee that he will take up some line, and though I may in a sense compel him to do so, I can never be quite sure what that line will be. His freedom is the concrete form of his independence from material determinism, and if there were not some indetermination in the reply, my action would not have been prayer. It would have been either an act that transcends human intercourse, i.e. a divine creation, or an act inferior to that intercourse, i.e. the play of a merely habitual or reflex mechanism.

Of course this connexion between the reply and the freedom of the individual comprises various forms that differ in quality. This may be equivalently expressed by saying that the reply depends upon an exercise of reason, but that, in order to do this, reason may appeal to maxims of greater or less nobility. If, for example, someone submits to the influence of a petitioner "for the sake of peace", or from self-interest, if he is seduced by a vendor's patter (or if he bases his refusal upon similar motives of pleasure or profit), he is choosing self-centred reason as his rule, and it would be more accurate to call it calculation than reason. But if justice or duty is his guide, the quality of his choice is more closely connected with true reason; reason becomes autonomous, i.e. it delivers him from his egoistic impulses. All this, Kant realised. But what perhaps he did not see is that reason is never more autonomous, and the personality never more reasonable than when true love is a factor. We have to accept the paradox that assent to the essential, undiluted reality of another person always leads to the discovery of the essence of one's own freedom. This is a curious encounter between necessity and initiative, passivity and the most original activity, the universality of the maxim (love thy neighbour as thyself) and the individuality of the decision.

In short, to be free means to have an implicit recourse to some form of reason; but when this reason only expresses an individual's reaction to the external world, then any decision he may take that concerns one of his fellows will be impure, inadequate or culpable; this is the case with hedonistic or utilitarian maxims in human intercourse. And in the logic of the passions freedom may to some extent even pervert reason. When, on the other hand, reason is the expression of a wisdom that belongs to the sphere of persons; when it takes into account the being of the other as of a creature who is himself capable of reason and of finding his place directly in the personal sphere; when, lastly, it admits that on account of this prerogative the other holds an eminent position in the visible cosmos, then reason becomes coincident with the finest activity of freedom; it is now not only the root of freedom, it enters into unity with it and gives it its highest value.

In the last analysis, the following proposition cannot be called irrational: a human being never answers a prayer addressed to him with more perfect freedom than when his decision is motivated by love. If he follows other motives, he undergoes the influence of the petitioner in a form which fails to give freedom to them both, and which, leaving him in his solitude, does not even completely free himself. Doubtless, one is independent and free with respect to a partner if one answers him in some rational way which remains extrinsic to him, but it is one thing to reject or even to adopt in a spirit of justice a suggestion which concerns a partial aspect of the petitioner, and a very different matter to welcome the man himself in an impulse of generous love. Only in this latter case do the two persons mutually fulfil each other in the same common purpose.

It follows from this that the decision involved in the reply may be based on the most divergent values and justify itself by reasons of very unequal worth. All the examples we have previously quoted

could be used again from this point of view in order to show the
different levels of the attitudes concerned (Hector answering Andromache, Achilles receiving Priam, the donor considering the beggar,
the nurse replying to the sick man, etc.). And it would be evident
that a single attitude is often inspired by several motives which are
far from being of equal value: it is the mixture that determines the
quality of an act, rather than the purity of a single motive, which is
really a rather illusory state.

The central difficulty of this chapter deserves a final confronta-
tion. Is it true or not that prayer is a resolve to move and alter the
will of another? Is it true or not that this resolve has an efficient
power? We answered these questions affirmatively inasmuch as the
person praying is engaged in a struggle (1) to secure the recognition
of his existence and its manifestation; (2) to establish the value, both
affective and rational, of his petition. We answered negatively, in so
far as the person praying observes and respects the other's freedom
of decision. In that case he will not be in conflict with him, but sometimes with himself and the vehemence of his own desires; sometimes
the shock administered by the answer he gets will move him to consider the amendment of his petition and to realise its defects.

This idea implies that the response always makes a real and active
contribution. The determinism of the outgoing influence, even
though it may succeed in inducing its recipient to agree that the
petition is well-grounded, cannot compel consent. For although I
may be convinced that you are right, I am not obliged to act on that
conviction; I may love or hate you, I may be indifferent, I may
resist you, I may be in two minds. Where does this restriction on
the outgoing influence originate? It arises from the fact that, as we
have seen, although the persons concerned may not be mentioned
in the statement of the purpose of the prayer, it will always be sub-
ordinated to them and, as it were, involved in their destiny. Now
the development of these persons is continuous and never-ending,
so that, *ipso facto*, the formal content of the prayer, the plea, becomes relative. Every prayer is incorporated in the mutual growth of
two personalities, and, hence, can never, in its form and purpose,

retain a character of absolute necessity; it has to come down from the abstract and *in se* to the concrete and *propter nos*. At this level demonstration becomes pleading, and it remains an open question whether the plea that best expresses my needs or yours, shall be accepted or not by me, your listener. For neither you nor I can be limited to the images of ourselves—whether indirect or direct— which your plea offers; we have already gone on ahead of them; we have to reach a definition of ourselves by ratifying, rejecting, or transforming the view you have presented.

You could, of course, compel me to agree, but if you did that, it would be by abolishing my mind; what you put forward would certainly not be a prayer, and what I said in return would not be a reply. Force can certainly compel men, but no force in the world can make of conduct that is entirely determined a free act. It is for this reason that to reply means to contribute an additional element which the petition alone cannot explain.

There are cases in which the continuity between petition and reply seems to be homogeneous, cases of spontaneous agreement. The request is no sooner made than granted. But although I may love you and although your petition harmonises perfectly with your welfare and mine, I still retain the freedom to find my own original way of answering you. No form of prayer exists, therefore, from the abject to the sublime, which does not involve in its development the activity of a twofold freedom.

This does not mean that an influence which is irresistibly effective and complete is blighted by some essential evil. The opposite is true, for to bestow its being upon a being is to create it and consequently to endow it with its most substantial good. But once this being has been created, and this creature become conscious, the influence exerted upon it cannot be that of the previous type. To try to reduce it to that would be anachronistic, absurd and criminal. The proper influence now can only be to move that being to an act of perception; it may perhaps also impose the necessity of coming to a decision, but it is not its business to decide what that decision shall be. In the order of interhuman relations neither creation by another nor self-positing by the individual is possible or desirable, but rather, mutual influence that combines a mutual power to affect necessarily, and also an individual freedom. It is as though the moment we have been given being by God, we make an initial act of self-affirmation by a decision of the will that is bound to be identical with that act. After that, however, we have to go on to develop our own being, that of others and God's lot in the world, through a form of intercourse which demands that each shall be responsible for all in such a way that, though his decision is great, it does not leave him isolated.[6] Prayer sets forth and manifests in the most striking way this intermediary régime of a collaboration at the level of man's inmost being. It enables a man to be by anticipation both what he himself can become and what another man also can become, while allowing each of the two who meet in prayer to retain his share of freedom in the action which they carry out together.

[6] In my *Personne humaine et nature*, Paris, 1963, Chap. 7, I suggested that these two forms of volition might be called original freedom (*liberté primitive*) and derived freedom (*liberté dérivée*).

CHAPTER 5

Hierarchical Relationships in Prayer

1. *Social Superiority*

As an approach to the subject of this chapter, let us once again turn to Homer. In Book 6 of the *Odyssey*, Ulysses, shipwrecked and naked, is awakened on the beach by the cries of Nausicaa and her attendants playing ball.

Odysseus considered whether he should throw his arms round the beautiful girl's knees and so make his prayer, or be content to keep his distance and beg her with all courtesy to give him clothing and direct him to the city. After some hesitation he decided that as the lady might take offence if he embraced her knees it would be better to keep his distance and politely plead his case.

The cunning man then speaks to the girl in words calculated to touch her feelings. He had quickly guessed that she was of noble birth; he calls her Queen, compares her to Artemis, remarks on the good fortune of her parents and of the man who would one day wed her. "Only in Delos have I seen the like, a fresh young palm-cone shooting up by the altar of Apollo." This memory enables him to allude unobtrusively to his own social rank. Next he tells the story of the misfortunes he has met at sea. Then comes the specific request, reduced to the strict minimum: Would she direct him to the town and give him some rags to cover himself? His speech, perfect in its conciseness and tact, concludes with an invocation to the gods to reward his benefactress and with good wishes for her future home.[1]

A passage like this at once reveals the affinities between prayer and social inferiority. Nausicaa issues orders to her servants; she is a

---

[1] *Odyssey*, 6, 85–197. [Rieu, pp. 106–7.]

princess. Ulysses is a poor devil, hungry and humiliated; he is a suppliant. The relationship, however, is more complex than at first appears. Ulysses is a man; his physical strength gives him a superiority over the weakness and emotionalism of the girls among whom he has arrived. But society has reversed this privilege by obliging men to observe the decencies and be courteous; it is woman who has the right to be considered superior, at least in social life, if not in public affairs. But Ulysses has other advantages to exploit: his very nakedness and his wild appearance thoroughly scare the modest maidens. He is also older than the adolescent to whom he speaks. And yet these various aids to immediate superiority are neutralised by his position, at once tragic and ridiculous, as a shipwrecked man; they would not have lasted for long, had the alarm been sounded in the town. He takes good care to keep out of his behaviour any suspicion of boldness; this would have been both incongruous and risky. True, he is a king, but he has lost his throne, and the only way to establish his rank is to exhibit a regal sensitivity. From all this, one fact emerges crystal clear: he is in an utter fix, and therefore the only thing he can do is to "pray" and to entrust himself to the first human being he meets, and to whom, according to the ideas of the time, he would be sacred: "Strangers, beggars, are all sent us by Zeus!"

From a social point of view, there can be no doubt about the fact that prayer proceeds from the inferior to the superior, whether it is a plea for life, for food or for protection. It can, therefore, easily include an element of flattery: "You have an outstanding character, I look upon you as a father, etc." The petitioner does humble himself, but he also manages to insinuate self-praise, by presenting an image in which destitution and nobility of nature are combined. He attempts to show, sometimes with more or less conscious exaggeration of the gulf between his merits and his lot, that he is more deserving of attention than anyone. This prayer is accompanied by promises of gratitude and devotion. Here also, there is exaggeration; not every suppliant has the moderation of a Ulysses, and in return for the slightest service many a man will promise boundless devotion. This is a somewhat contemptible way of substituting a quasi-contract for genuine prayer and of establishing a commercial equality with gain as its inspiration.

All this amounts to an unpleasant mixture of sincerity, hypocrisy and servility. In a society where the leaders enjoy a power in striking contrast to the wretchedness of the people, obsequiousness is the rule, and this produces hyperbole which in the end penetrates even into the sphere of family and friendly relationships.

Happily, there are exceptions to this, as the example of the sublime Ulysses shows. Also, a hierarchical ordering of society does not necessarily create an atmosphere of pathological cringing. An inferior can always express himself with a certain pride. Haydn, for example, was a dependant, wearing the livery of the Esterhazys, and yet when he wanted to make Count Nicholas conclude an interminable season and allow his musicians to go home, he thought out a plan that was both symbolical and elegant. He composed his *Farewell Symphony*, in which the musicians leave the orchestra one after another, each having first extinguished the candle at his music-stand; at last only two violins are left and the conductor walks off too. The count took the hint and released them all next day. Dry humour is extremely effective.

At a deeper level than that of such ingenious methods, we should note, finally, that subordinates regain a superior status through the very act of praying. The leader's command, as such, has no concern with the degree of freedom of the person commanded and no interest in an exchange of views; but prayer is addressed directly to a person who is free to deliberate and decide. It belongs to the mature phase of human intercourse and begins with a dialogue of two conscious selves. That is why its development is the sign of an entrance into civilisation. It is the petitioner who enters it first, because, by reason of his very impotence, he makes an appeal to the clear-sightedness or kindliness of the man who holds sway over him and could crush him.

Mankind has always instinctively realised these things. It has realised also that fortune is unstable and that the victors of today may well be the exiles and beggars of tomorrow. This explains why among many races the suppliant is held to be sacred and thus gains an unexpected superiority which protects him against attack. Profoundly moving regulations direct him to be treated with respect; they resemble the laws of hospitality, indeed when they speak of the refuge one should give to a hunted man, they are identical with them. This is one of the favourite themes of classical drama. In Sophocles' *Oedipus at Colonus*, Theseus says to the aged exile: "I could not refuse assistance to any stranger coming as you come. I am too well aware that I also am a man and that I do not dispose of tomorrow." But Creon does his utmost to get round the law of the gods, not scrupling even to violate it brutally. Moreover, outside the protecting territory the supplication no longer availed and a death sentence regained its rights. Stricken mankind! How hard it finds the task of extricating itself from its primaeval clay! In spite of appearances, it has never ceased to apply illegitimate and savage solutions to its cases of conscience.

2. *Psychological and Moral Superiority*

The hierarchy created by strength and force affords an insufficient basis for prayer. Very early another formative factor appeared, that of intellectual and moral superiority. This is evident from the fact that flattery so often pays homage to competence or virtue. It is not only the power of the great that the suppliant extols, it is also their spirit of initiative, justice and generosity.

It was not long, however, before these two hierarchies became divided; the mortar of flattery does not bind and incense has never had the power to bestow genius or competence upon anyone who lacks it. Hence it is that in order to obtain sound spiritual advice one would sometimes prefer an unknown curate to a cardinal, and for stomach trouble, one would not consult a chiropodist. At the very least, we can say that the social hierarchy splits up and that a multitude of superiorities is produced that lodge together, in the same individual, with inferiorities that are no less blatant: the President of the French Republic asks for the assistance of the humblest railwayman when he travels by train, and yet expects every one to reverse their parts and to stand to attention when he steps out of his carriage. And it may happen that I have the very lowest possible opinion of the private life of a surgeon to whom, on account of his ability, I do not hesitate to entrust my life, in preference to any other. In this way each of us becomes the recipient of certain requests as a result of a restricted and transitory privilege; daily life consists of an alternating series of prayers that makes us pass with amazing speed from the function of petitioner to that of donor, or inversely.

Must we deduce from this that in prayer, superiority is, by definition, recognised as belonging to its recipient, and that he thereby possesses what may be called a greater richness of being than his petitioner? In a sense, we must. But there are cases for which this hardly holds, when the inferiority of the suppliant is so conventional that it deceives no one. It is a flimsy and transparent veil that permits the true proportions of the persons present to be grasped at first sight.

The fundamental example of this is to be found in the situation created by "prayer" between friends. Its formal setting of question and response never really conceals the radical equality in the relationship. For the real basis of friendship is mutual service; when I ask you for something, I have it in mind to do something similar in return for you. And although unfortunate circumstances may prevent me from providing this, it is understood that one day, if I have the means, I shall make up what I owe. All friendship includes this tendency to synchronise, I was going to say "eternalise" its mutual petitions. Apart from those cases where friends find it easy to break away from their social antecedents, there are obviously many others that call for balancing feats of no mean skill if real harmony is to be achieved. A sympathetic master, for example, who feels an affection towards an old and faithful servant, ceases to issue commands; instead he makes respectful requests, whose courteous phrases sometimes seem to reverse their relationship. An aged nurse is treated with as much respect and affection as a grandmother. The difference in social position is annulled by respectful consideration.

There is another series of prayers which in their development produce real or apparent exceptions to the hierarchical relationship of those concerned in them. These are prayers of intercession.

The petitioner addresses a mediator. This latter is traditionally thought of as occupying a position midway between the petitioner and the ultimate donor. The definition, however, is inadequate. The mediator, or, if the term is preferred, the intercessor, may be superior to the person with whom the final decision lies. A cousin of a minister of state asks him to recommend a departmental head. Perhaps even, the cousin may not have made any request; the minister, being a good-hearted fellow, took the initiative. It was not an order, but a wish; the difference may seem subtle and may provoke a smile; it is, however, real enough. In the unending chain of intercessions which bind men together, not everything can be reduced to shady practices, to attempts at bribery and pulling wool over people's eyes. Delicate interconnexions of self-interests can be thoroughly sound on account of their object and their method. It may or may not be edifying, but for the psychologist the process offers, in its simplest pattern, the characteristic feature of two quasi-egalitarian "prayers" that take the place of a single "prayer" in which the divorce between those concerned was too great: my friend's friend does not become my friend, but the result is the same as if he were my friend; without this transference of influence he would only be a remote terminus and the barrier between him and me would be impassable. Sometimes the distance is vertical, but when this is not so, it involves the same obstacles and demands the same remedies. For example, I am not conscious of being inferior in the social, psychological or moral hierarchy to a New York or Moscow publisher, but I shall certainly obtain the books I need more easily if I have a friend on the spot.

Lastly, there is a series of prayers which not only complicates the hierarchical relationship, but seems to overturn and pervert it deliberately. We might call this series that of "prayer to the profligate". When Burrhus throws himself at Nero's feet and begs him not to smirch his reign by an infamous crime, where, from the moral point of view, does the superiority reside? "If you are about to commit so black a deed, sir, here am I, ready; before you leave, transfix this heart which cannot consent to it."

A change of roles is also to be encountered in the less dramatic but more habitual "prayer" with which parents offer good advice to their children. The child is not guilty, but is in danger of becoming so; its father and mother have more experience and are presumed to possess moral stability. They consider that in the circumstances they should, not command a given line of conduct, but recommend it; so their "prayer" will respect the autonomy which belongs to their growing son or daughter. No one would consider that they lower themselves in doing so.

In all these cases, the superiority attached to the person who is addressed springs from his independence as a free being; he is seen as possessing a unique value of which he is the master. It is a remarkable fact that a prayer offered to another for his good—the most disinterested form of petition—always implies that a nobler personality humbles itself before a man who is unstable or even contemptible and points to some great reality within him. Everything else is forgotten; the luminous point alone shines out. The reason for this is not simply my hope that the criminal will listen to me and be converted (prayer made in that spirit might well be pharisaical), but that from this moment I give him back an element of honour, I acclaim some real integrity in him which others, and he himself, have not seen, and which prayer alone has the power to discover and contemplate.

3. *Soliloquy and the Hierarchic Division within the Self*
In classical times the Stoics sometimes transferred the cult of the good "genius" to a cult of the ideal self. According to an inscription of the third century B.C., Posidonius and his disciples in Halicarnassus decided to sacrifice a ram on the first day of the month of Hermes to the ἀγαθὸς δαίμων of Posidonius himself. "Here then", remarks Erwin Rohde, "offering is made to the ἀγαθὸς δαίμων of the living, just as offering was made on birthdays, and at other times also, to the *genius* of Romans; ἀγ. δ. is here clearly equivalent to *genius*." This particular δαίμων of the individual, who might appear to him (as, according to Plutarch, Brutus' κακὸς δαίμων appeared to him) was not considered, even in popular belief, to be the soul itself. But for the Stoics it was "'the original, ideal personality as

contrasted with the empirical personality'. . . . the character the man already *is* ideally, but must *become* actually". Thus the δαίμων which is different from the διάνοια becomes identical with it. In the thought of Marcus Aurelius the δαίμων is indistinguishable from the individual mind and forms the ultimate perfection of our personality.[2] St Augustine also frequently addresses himself in his *Confessions*: "Do not be foolish, O my soul."[3] But in his theory, unlike that of Marcus Aurelius, the process is one of descent: the higher soul speaks to the lower in order to exhort and convert it. Sometimes this latter is personified in a deed: "What then did wretched I so love in thee, O theft of mine, thou deed of darkness, in that sixteenth year of my age? Lovely thou wert not, because thou wert theft. But art thou anything at all, that thus I speak to thee?"[4] It would be interesting to find out whether this apostrophe is Neo-platonic in origin and whether the rhetoric whose purpose is to raise the lower self on the wings of words to its higher originating principle, is not following a path symmetrical with that of the divine visitation which occurs in ecstasy.

Is a soliloquy a prayer? Or is it just a literary artifice? Ordinarily, it is assumed to be the latter. This makes things easy and disposes elegantly of a mysterious fact—the absence of unity in our self, condemned as it is to divide into two quasi-personalities and to oscillate between two poles. It is true, of course, that "prayer" to oneself is a fiction, inasmuch as the I that prays cannot be cleanly separated

---

[2] E. Rohde, *Psyche*. The Cult of Souls and Belief in Immortality among the Greeks, London, 1925, pp. 514–15. On this point the author quotes and accepts the conclusions of Bonhöffer.

[3] *Confessions*, 4, 11, 1.

[4] Ibid., 2, 6, 1. Elsewhere, however, he speaks to his memory as God's dwelling-place, or again, to the human soul in general ("*Videamus ergo, o anima humana, utrum praesens tempus possit esse longum; datum enim tibi est sentire moras atque metiri. Quid respondebis mihi?*" 11, 15, 19. Cf. 10, 6, 10; 10, 24, 34, etc.). Note also, at the beginning of the *Soliloquies*, the voice within him he heard telling him to pray to God, without his being able to discover its origin ("*sive ego ipse, sive alius quis extrinsecus sive intrinsecus, nescio*").

Thus prayer to oneself, in the thought of Augustine, is intrinsically complex; sometimes it is an upward, sometimes a downward movement, sometimes neither of these, but simply a matter of question and answer, or of the pursuit of ideas; and, sometimes, the voice of another being who speaks to us or to whom we speak.

from the I to which the prayer is addressed; the otherness is not an external one, and so, in this sense, the separation is not complete. But under cover of the self that prays is it not the voice of another that is making itself heard? This would provide an explanation of the experiences of temptation, of inspiration, of yearning, of the inner dialogue between God or the devil and ourselves, or quite simply the voice of absent ones, the living or the dead.

Conscience is presumed to be the voice of God; it speaks for him, and perhaps for others also. To some extent it may be felt to be something outside us which enters into us, becomes part of our substance and of the spontaneous expression of our being. Each influence it receives is then expressed outwardly: this voice we hear within us as our own refers us, in the last resort, to others beyond ourselves. It awakens us to ourselves in order that we may awaken ourselves to others. We do not know where what we have received originated and yet only by returning to its origins can it reach perfection.

It is, therefore, easy to understand that the conversations that occur in spiritual writers (in the *Imitation*, for example), are often such that we cannot tell whether the writer is speaking to himself or to the reader, or whether it is God who is presumed to be speaking. This ambiguity is natural and shows that in "prayer" addressed to the self we are approaching the territory of "the holy". A soliloquy is not always a prayer; but even should we insist on giving it a homely and amusing form, it cannot fail to make us conscious of something quite extraordinary (*I* is someone else). When, however, the soliloquy has really become a prayer, then a new factor suggests itself, a mystery it cannot express and from which it never escapes.

CHAPTER 6

The Element of "The Holy" in Inter-human Prayer

Whenever an imprudent hand attempted to remove the veil from the goddess Isis, an awareness of "the holy" was experienced, for it is precisely this drawing near to something that is final in the order of being that quickens this awareness. It is true, of course, that not every event which contains something beyond the here and now is sacred. For instance, every meeting between separate beings involves a reality deeper than mere contact, and yet such meetings are often trivial and nothing essential is expected from them. Even when we are menaced by some threat, when our life, for example, is endangered, it is not the physical agent as such that provokes the terror of "the holy"; *that* is the result of what underlies the action, and is produced because suddenly the very substance of my being is at stake and will yield up its secret as it dies. From the moral point of view, danger may be the circumstance which favours a similar revelation, or, it may be the sign that I have been abruptly thrown into an alien realm of being in which I am ill at ease. The mystery of my being, that of others, the mystery of being itself, is about to reveal itself. I had not been thinking about it, and yet I feel it to be so. The irresistible awareness of "the holy" comes about in this way.

It is never neutral. It is existential in a double sense, first because it gives the alarm about some concrete, individual being who confronts me—who I may even be myself—and second, because, if the alarm is given on one point, it is given on all. The "holy" overthrows the even tenor of existence; even when its message is peace, it first produces fear. And then, because it is a meeting or an approach to a meeting, the being who is responsible for it is regarded as a speaker or as one who can be spoken to. There is a relationship between "the holy" and prayer.

"The holy" has many forms, and for the moment we are not concerned with enumerating them.[1] But they can be divided into two quite distinct classes; one which ascends direct to God; the other is imbedded among men. In this latter case we must distinguish between a "holy" that would be the perfection of a created being and that which would disintegrate and pervert it; the former leads to a divine condition, the latter to diabolical activity.

Nothing forbids us *a priori* to hold that God wishes us to become divine. But if we become devilish God is excluded and our divinisation may be achieved in such a way that it leads practically or theoretically to that result. Such is the case with idolatry.

Prayer between human beings leaves room for the "holy", and we will first examine the idolatrous mode it can well adopt and then the divinisation that could be its end to the exclusion of idolatry.

1. *Idolatrous Prayer*

Idolatry lurks at a thousand corners to pervert human prayer. First it seeks an entry through the gates of social life. The courtier tries to concentrate his whole personal prayer upon the leader; he is a specialist in petition. Less intelligently, but more nobly, the partisan is a specialist in devotion, self-effacing in a common supplication to the leader. In his attitude the element of petition decreases, but the element of fanaticism increases and makes the idolatry more absolute. The leader ceases to be the source of plans and policies and becomes a divinity who is blessed even when he slays. The fanatic is religious, the courtier is not. The fanatic is a danger to his leader's adversaries because he is wholly committed to the task in hand. The courtier is a danger to his leader because self-interest lies behind his prayer; in his case the integrity of prayer is not sincerely maintained. Egoistic petition leads irresistibly to hypocrisy, the moment some slight divergence between the immediate interests of the partners occurs. For, in fact, the courtier despises his official idol and his real object of worship is himself. The fanatic's

[1] I may refer to my book, *Conscience et Logos*, Paris, 1961, pp. 110ff.

idolatry, on the other hand, is essentially noble; it makes a man a hero through his own devotion to a hero.

But when a man realises that he may be the subject of a cult, a new pathway to idolatry is opened up. It is very different from the vulgar narcissism in which one contemplates one's bodily features in a mirror. Its foundation lies in the pride of some technical achievement: "I have killed the Nemean lion and cleansed the Augean stables, revere me." The cult of the hero situates its object midway between God and man; the Greeks practised it, the Romans were less interested.[2] Whether or not it is fully idolatrous, it is for the most part the joint creation of the hero who blows up his personality by parading all his achievements and of his admirers who allow themselves to be captivated by his beauty, power and virtue and have eyes for none but the bearer of these qualities. Posthumous idealisation does the rest.

This is the element of truth in euhemerism, and the Fathers of the Church usually interpreted the origins of paganism in this way.

> Our ancestors [remarks Minucius Felix] were unenlightened, credulous and childish with regard to the gods. They payed religious honour to their kings, after their death they sought to retain their presence in paintings and their memory in statues, with the result that what was at first a comfort soon became a religion. Moreover, before the world was opened up by commercial intercourse . . . each nation worshipped its own founder, a leader of renown, a chaste queen, triumphing over her sex, or the inventor of some art, some benefit to man, as a citizen to be remembered with appropriate honour. In this way the dead received their reward and an example was provided for those still to be born.[3]

The approaches giving access to private idolatry are not so very different, and the main way is sexual love. The two concerned in it

---

[2] The Homeric gods are involved in the visible cosmos and are not very distinct from men. They are certainly deathless, but they can be injured, and when they refresh men with the divine nectar men become almost unconquerable. The boundary between the divine hero and the gods in the strict sense is very vague. Among the Romans it is more clearly marked, with notable exceptions (Romulus and Remus) and a development (Julius Caesar) hastened by the divinisation of the emperors.

[3] Minucius Felix, *Octavius*, 20. CSEL, 2, pp. 28–9. Cf. *Dictionnaire de Théologie catholique*, Art. "Idolâtrie", col. 652.

shut out the world, and make themselves the universe. Each ascribes to his partner the privileges of God. The element of petition decreases, and absolute admiration and devotion increase, at least in principle. This it is which endows the idolatry of love with its nobility, and relegates the error of Narcissus to the lowest place, for Narcissus only prays to a shadow of himself, and that is the final degradation.

Whatever the sphere may be, idolatry supervenes when prayer is confined to some secondary aspect of the being to whom it is addressed, goes on then to eliminate every being but this particular one, just as it eliminates in the beloved object everything except this one aspect, and lastly comes to hold the being regarded with such poverty of vision as the absolute source of value. St Thomas Aquinas adds a further interesting element to this definition: he distinguishes between "perfect" idolatry which consists in a genuine belief that some created being is God, and "imperfect" but far more perverse idolatry which is not unaware of God's reality and rights, and yet pretends to be, and from hatred of the Creator bows down before the creature.[4]

In its early chapters the Old Testament provides us with a notion of what an idol is that is seemingly much more material: Yahweh prohibits the carving of images in wood and stone. In reality, the prohibition includes much more than this, for it forbade men to make any work of art. It was not only Yahweh of whom a representation must not be made, but also men and animals and any created thing. Behind this austerity relative to worship there lies a profound idea: we have an unruly impulse to attribute an exaggerated importance to the work of our hands. *Homo faber* becomes a prisoner of his own skills; he puts himself in the place of his Creator and uses the instruments he has made as the measure of reality. This biblical standpoint also enables us to perceive that there are degrees in idolatry. Passionate admiration or love for another does not constitute the worst form of atheism, for it is very difficult to dodge the problem of God in the heart of another man, and however slight the element of reality I adore may be, it still can serve to raise me to the

[4] DTC, col. 668–9.

stars. Real paganism is enslavement to technique; this quickly does away with prayer between men and even with the Stoic or Neoplatonic soliloquy; all that is left to confront us is a machine; having dried up the sense of mystery, it sucks us into itself. The idol we have fashioned depopulates heaven and earth and reduces its worshippers to dumbness.

When the Positivists proposed that we should worship mankind they muddled together two very different forms of enthusiasm. In their catechism we read: "For us, prayer becomes the ideal of life. For prayer is at once love and thought and even action." One of their members used this noble sentence as an introduction to a curious collection of prayers which he composed for every day of the week. "Sacred mankind, our mother and benefactress," he exclaims.[5] Such invocations would not probably have aroused the sternest anger of the prophets of Israel. That would have been provoked by the claim that man is not a created being and that he is to be loved solely for his material achievements, his "victory over nature".

2. Divinising Prayer

At the beginning of the Book of Genesis, the serpent promises Adam and Eve that they shall be as gods. In Psalm 81 [82], Yahweh declares: "Ye are gods; and ye are all children of the Most High." This title has been accepted literally by Christianity. It follows from this that, in one sense, idolatry does not consist in the divinisation of man in Christian tradition, for that tradition teaches man's divine vocation more imperatively than did the Greek tradition. It may impose heavier obligations than did the Greeks, but it raises no objection in principle to the possibility of our divinisation. The idea that there is a limit to what we may expect from the rational creature must be rejected by genuine Christian belief. From man we may ask all things, hope for all things, provided that we do not separate him from grace, i.e. from the supreme will of his Creator, and from the scheme of the created world. Idolatry does not consist in an excessive contemplation and love of our fellows; on the contrary, it

[5] J. Longchampt, *Essai sur la prière*. Paris, 1853.

consists in not contemplating them enough and in loving them too little or in the wrong way.

When any being comes to be associated with God it acquires a kind of eternal sufficiency of which it would be incapable on its own. This absolute, inexhaustible potentiality is so indispensable to prayer, for a Christian, that he would consider a God who could not contain in himself the whole weight of his own creation, and who denied it, to be an idol. If we abandon one attribute of God and single out another, we transform him into a false God. Even truth can be made into an idol, said Pascal.

Consequently we must take our stand against an age-old tradition that has afflicted Christianity, probably coming from Neoplatonism, and that makes of created beings a mere reflexion or temporary dwelling-place of the divinity. All we can ask from them, on this view, is that they send us on our way towards God. We find this outlook as early as Origen: he considered that we should not pray to "any being that has been produced", not even to Christ, but to the Father alone. This depreciation of temporal values is compensated, in his thought, by the value he puts on freedom, but only partially. "It was a task for the disciples of Jesus that they cross to the other bank, that they rise above the visible and corporeal for it lasts but a moment, and hasten towards the invisible and eternal."[6] The universe is simply a training ground and matter a temporary garment, which one must learn to do without in order to return to God. St Paul's point of view would appear to have been less unbalanced: all creatures can acquire their true, organic relationship within the mystery of God; they are not reduced to playing the part of mirrors. When ecclesiastical spirituality has yielded on occasion to this nostalgia for the supreme One, as interpreted by more or less simplified commentaries on Plato, Plotinus and Pseudo-Dionysius, it has lost one of the deepest and most original lessons of the gospel. It has turned away from the world and from human intercourse, as though that multiplicity had to be forsaken as we mount Godwards, instead of being divinely redeemed and maintained.

Prayer between human beings has a permanent place in any

[6] Origen, *In Matthaeum*, 11, 5. GCS, p. 41.

Christian teaching on prayer, that is, if it is true that the command-
ment to love our neighbour is akin to that of loving God. Its special
place is in intercession and sacrifice. The hope of divinisation was
not erroneous; the falsehood lay in claiming that we could achieve
this by ourselves.

Florence Nightingale wrote a sentence, disturbingly equivocal,
but which will bear a sound interpretation: "God's scheme for us
is not that He should give us what we ask for, but that mankind
should obtain it for mankind."[7] On such a view a completely god-
less society could be built, and prayer to God be lost in prayer to
man. This is the dangerous aspect of the statement. But, on the
other hand, is it not true that prayer between human beings is one
of the possible climaxes of divine charity, and that it is the latter that
confers its full value on the former? Is it not in the movement by
which human prayer acquires its highest quality that it is led to
discover its origins and its horizons in God? Goethe felt this transition very keenly in that crisis of love which has left us the *Marienbad
Elegy*: "In the pure centre of our soul there stirs the desire to give
ourselves spontaneously and thankfully to some higher, purer being,
unknown to us, a desire decoding for itself the eternally unnamed
being. This feeling we call piety. This is the blessed height I feel
I have attained when I stand before her."[8] Instead of the ancient
obsecratio which aimed at magically bringing down some heavenly
power into the petition addressed to another human being, we now
have the spirit of love which can maintain the human dialogue without fictitious aids, and make it intrinsically religious, until it becomes
an appeal to God and a confession of his transcendence.

It was rejection and suffering that made the aging Goethe feel the
religious *aura* of his beloved. Absence—physical or moral—which
disturbs or interrupts human intercourse, often leads us to the

[7] Quoted by H. E. Fosdick, *The Meaning of Prayer*, vi, Third Day, Sixth
Week. Fontana, p. 114.
[8] *In unsers Busens Reine wogt ein Streben*
Sich einem Höhern, Reinern, Unbekannten
Aus Dankbarkeit freiwillig hinzugeben,
Enträtselnd sich den ewig Ungennanten;
Wir heissen's: fromm sein!—Solcher seligen Höhe
Fühl' ich mich teilhaft, wenn ich vor ihr stehe.

discovery of its most mysterious realms, as though the deprivation of something easily obtainable opened the gate to values harder to obtain and made us more worthy to receive them. Even if we allow "the holy" to retain its ambiguity of being either diabolical or divine, we can still demonstrate this change of level with reference to the lyrical outpourings of poetic address in love.

The secret prayer addressed to someone absent brings a sacred intensity to the memory of his face, and poetic worth to the thoughts it brings to mind. A photograph, too, is something more than a material likeness: it condenses and transforms the forces of affection. Silence and distance are dramatic episodes that do not always cause forgetfulness; in souls capable of it, they produce a lyrical change. The transition from drama to lyricism is an immediate impoverishment of action, but in literature, as in life, it enables us to reach deeper elements in our own being and in that of others.

Another instructive example is that of prayer offered to the dead. In this case the suppression of corporeal dialogue works for its sublimation. The relationship between those concerned is more subtle than before death, but none the less real. The survivor speaks to the dead friend and receives from him a message without alloy; it may happen that some intention, formerly misunderstood, is suddenly seen in its true perspective.

Is this surprising? It should not be, for the more religious a prayer becomes, the more it escapes from the control of the senses. As we approach the problem of prayer addressed to God, we leave this realm of visual and auditory dialogue, the stage proper to prayer between human beings. Now the common ground of prayer has ceased to be essentially material; it includes our human weakness, but it originates in a Being who is above and beyond all our categories.

Part Two

PRAYER AS ADDRESSED TO GOD

The Radical Difference between Divine and Human Prayer

In the preface we said that our starting-point is our own religious experience, and that, with few exceptions, we shall not refer to Buddhism or Confucianism. The God who will be discussed in this chapter will be the God common to Jews, Christians and Mohammedans. There are, of course, differences in interpretation, but for our purpose these will be disregarded, and God will be taken as meaning the God of our traditional theism. When we enquire what radically new element enters into prayer to this God, as compared with prayer to human beings, the following remarks at once suggest themselves.

1. *The Person now Addressed is not an Object of Sense*

(1) We learn from the history of religions that men have constantly tried to reach God either through the senses that demand some external object (sight, hearing), or, more frequently and in a way one may be allowed to think more moving, through those senses that involve participation, such as taste and sexual intercourse (hence sacred meals and sacred prostitution). And yet this untiring effort, which the great religions have incorporated and transformed in their sacraments, is, considered in itself alone, vain and permanently hopeless. God may indeed be found in an operation in which the senses have their part to play, but he himself is not a physical datum. It is also true that some men may receive visions and have auditory experiences, or feel themselves to be almost organically one with a being greater than themselves, but this does not alter the fact that the normal conditions, the factors that specify the position of a man in prayer are absence in space (not vision) and silence (not conver-

sation), a separation as far as sensory perception is concerned. One can neither see, hear, taste nor touch the essence of God.

It may indeed be said that neither can the essence of a human being be known through the knowledge of the senses alone; it is the mind that grasps the root principle of all things, including matter. But between matter and sensible objects there is an intrinsic relationship, and between the human person and matter there is also something essential, whereas the connexion between the divine reality and the physical order is utterly different. There is no such union between God and matter as exists between soul and body. God is not bound to this world in any way at all. We realise at once that he is absolutely beyond the range of the senses. This does not mean that he is not present to matter and in all things, but that he is their master and, in this respect, as far removed as possible from matter and all things.

The *Peri Euches*, wrongly attributed to Aristotle, affirms that God is "either spirit or something beyond spirit".[1] In reality, however, the antithesis between God and matter does not consist in the fact that God is spirit; it lies in the fact that God is absolute independence or transcendence. It is because matter has in itself no wealth of values that God is its contrary; it is not because contact with matter would contaminate him.

(2) As a result of this, the relation between God and the physical world is unique in kind and has no adequate counterpart in any other relationship between beings. I can only pray to God *per ea quae facta sunt* if I realise that these *ea quae facta sunt* are symbols to be transcended, and are entirely transitory receptacles of the divine being. They do not form the substratum of that being; they are the substratum of events penetrated by his purposeful activity, the servants of his creative or redeeming aims. Prayer which makes the material universe its starting-point must, necessarily, comprise a poet's vision, for if God is seen in material things, if they provide the impetus that will land us at his feet, this means that they are

---

[1] "ἢ νοῦς ἐστιν ἢ ἐπέκεινά τι τοῦ νοῦ", quoted by E. Desplaces, "La Prière des philosophes grecs", in *Gregorianum*, vol. 41, 2 (April 1960), pp. 253–73.

being transfigured, because we are then sensing dimly in them the final stages in a whole history of creation. The great authority for this teaching is, as we have seen, Origen; but Teilhard de Chardin has retained its best elements, although, as against Origen, he endows matter with a deep reality and worth.

Whatever the ultimate destiny of matter may be, whether evaporation or condensation, it becomes, when we pray, a sign we immediately grasp and not an allegory for learned interpretation. Now a sign is not a part of a being, but a result of its activity or a conclusion drawn from its presence. A better way of describing it would be: a disclosure of one being within another, a presence made manifest through transparency.

When I "pray" to a man, his face is both a part of his body and a sign of his soul; when I pray to God, I cannot say that the face of this world is a part or a substratum of some sort of divine body; the created world simply and solely provides me with a sign of God: I try to welcome a purpose or to guess at it within the narrow limits of an event and this event's structure.

(3) This removal of every kind of sensible support is at once the great innovation and the great test of religion. God can only be envisaged through a kind of death to the world; the world abides as the indispensable means for getting beyond it, but it must be looked at not as supporting something, but as expressing something: the world does not support God, indeed the reverse is true. It is difficult to make such a change in one's point of view, but if it is not made, God may come to seem a stranger. Is not reality what we see, what we touch? Or, if it is something inward, is it not our own scrutiny of what takes place within us? God is outside a world conceived of in this way, outside such interior dialogues, and once we cease to consider external and internal realities as signs of God, once we have eliminated from them any other presence shining through their transparency, we become atheists, however much we may verbally deny it. Every human being has to undergo the shock of an apparent absence on God's part. The temptation is to conclude: God is nothing, since he cannot be perceived as created beings can be perceived and especially since he does not occupy the foreground of

life's thronged arena. Many minds fall to this temptation. It seems to them that the tangible world can well dispense with everything intangible and requires nothing but itself for its own existence and development, and for the sustenance of its constituent elements. "Let us look after our own garden." God is an intruder, a superfluous ghost; prayer is a soliloquy, an imaginary conversation addressed to emptiness.

Moreover, if we turn to the imagination and ask: Where is God? it can only answer: God is in the void. (This is not true, but what other testimony can the imagination possibly give on God?) Or again, imagination might indeed go to the other extreme and produce an hallucination; but this error is no better than the other, for in thus exalting the underlying image of the sign, it is God himself that the imagination is in danger of materialising.

The burning bush, for ever on fire, does indeed possess a striking efficacy as a revelation, but the danger of the bush's being worshipped is no less great than that of the divinity's being thrust far out into the void. It may be said against this that miracles do in fact occur and that the burning bush of Moses was one of them. But a miracle itself would cease to have any religious value if it confined God to a sign: to understand miracle in this way would be to degrade God. In the end it would mean the end of the sign as signification and, consequently, the end of the miracle.

For St Bonaventure "every creature is divine word because it proclaims God".[2] This idea suggests three strands in the language of prayer. First, the created being envisaged by the believing mind refers him to God; secondly, God, through this created being, expresses something of himself to the believing mind; and, thirdly, the believing mind makes its response to God through the sign it has received from him. Let us examine this response. In it we observe at once that the contemplative element of prayer addressed to God pursues a twofold course: the created being is looked at and seen, but in such a way that it is something pertaining to God that is

---

[2] "*Verbum divinum est omnis creatura quia Deum loquitur.*" *Com. in Ecclesiasten*, I, in the Quaracchi edition, 1893, vol. 6, p. 16. Cf. J. Bougerol, *Introduction à l'étude de saint Bonaventure*, Paris, 1961, p. 194.

aimed at (doubtless as a result of what St Bonaventure would call a "cotuition", rather than an intuition). Is this twofold course also pursued in the case of prayer between human beings? In a sense it is, for the outward material element of a man must be penetrated in order to reach the free centre of his personal decisions to which the prayer is addressed, but, in another sense, his outward material element even when transfigured, remains a part of him; it forms part of an ideal totality which is, as it were, anticipated by the vision held of him by the one who prays to him and whose request is directed towards the divine state of him to whom he prays. The case of prayer addressed to God is different, for God is not simply the divine state of a created being. No doubt it is true that when I pray to God the opaque character of some external or internal event is illuminated and I rise beyond the prosaic condition of the created being I am contemplating. But the twofold course in my contemplation becomes essentially divided, for it carries me beyond the poetic condition of the created being, or, more accurately, that condition becomes for me the mediator of a unique relationship whose end is entirely transcendent, apart from and independent of all created beings.

The mental attitude in which all this takes place is that of the vocative, and any prayer that is not in the vocative would be an absurdity; it would have no meaning. But if we now suppose that prayer has become chilled and has disappeared, then, when this happens, contemplation ceases and the created being which had become a sign falls back into its own particularised entity; and even if I still regard it poetically, I am no longer regarding God through it; at that precise moment the sign has become a symbol. The second person has been changed to the third; prayer has slipped into meditation. A symbol is either the residue or the precursor of prayer. It is a state in which an object has become separated from the reality it signifies and that had been invoked through it, and yet is still polarised by this reality. It is vague because it has lost connexion and to some extent direction also. It is this that makes it appear to be merely an abstraction derived from the object on which it rests. But it is not entirely artificial, since it is an expression of the obediential potency of all things existing in the world, an obediential potency that is a fundamental aspect of the contingent nature of every individual being.

A symbol is midway between the signifying function of the world of prayer, and the objective inter-connexion of the phenomena that make up the universe. Hence its serviceability in the systems of expression such as art and science.[3]

In divine, as distinct from human prayer, we have observed a profound alteration in the element of contemplation. There is a corresponding and even more pronounced change in petition and devotion. My requests and offerings are not now made to a created being; I forget all about it and turn to its Creator. In contemplation, the sign, of course, plays its part as a permanent spring-board or isthmus; but he whom I beseech and to whom I make my offering is the Ultimate in his unveiled majesty. The mediating created being (whether it is an external reality or an interior state of soul) is the object of my petition or devotion only in the sense that I use it to cannon off. Were it otherwise, prayer would fall into universal confusion; God's uniqueness would no longer respect that with which he endows his creatures, and neither would it be respected itself.

2. *God, Unlike the Human Beings to whom we Pray, is not Subject to Fate*

We come to a second essential difference. We noted above that even a hero's will is restricted: Hector was the captive of a psychological and social situation; he was metaphysically conditioned; Andromache's tears were powerless to alter this in any way. He could not

---

[3] In this paragraph *sign* is used in the sense of an activity between two subjects, as when we say that someone "makes a sign" to us; *symbol* is used objectively, with no reference to any mutual activity, although its content retains an element of flexibility. From these should be distinguished the *semanteme* or completely fixed and codified sign that exists in quantities in the various developed languages (those of gesture, of ordinary intercourse, those used in mathematics, etc.) and which fill the dictionaries. There exists, however, an intermediary between the symbol and the semanteme as thus explained: it is the idea or image which selects one aspect of a symbol in isolation from others and incorporates it in a systematic language.

pay attention to his wife alone, he could not become exclusively hers, or, rather, he could become everything to her only by refusing to stay with her at that moment, for, had he stayed, that would have made him a coward. He had to take a number of things into consideration: what his fellow soldiers expected of him, his civic responsibilities, his destiny which Zeus had settled or recorded.

When I pray to God, the person to whom I pray is not a Hector. He is dependent upon no one and he has no master. He has no superior and no equal. No third person can supervise the relations between my Creator and myself. He has no one to reckon with and fate obeys him.

This creates an entirely new situation for the suppliant. Religious prayer, we pointed out above, arises in the soul outside this world. We can now add that it is directed to God without any fear of the world. That is why it is our supreme resort. The only refuge that nothing can assail is God, the object of my prayer, and to this refuge I myself belong to the extent to which my life and prayer are one, and, when, so to speak, I myself have become a prayer. The being whom I address is the Almighty; I can add nothing to him, for even if he have any supplement or complement, it is still his will that produces it.

The Greeks found it difficult to accept the idea that the Father of the Gods was the absolute lord of all destiny. He was only relatively its master, a position befitting the strongest power in the world. In the Iliad, Zeus tells the assembled gods to suspend a golden rope from heaven, take hold of it and try to drag him down. He declares that the attempt will prove a lamentable failure; it is he who will drag them up. "If I cared to take a hand and pulled in earnest from my end, I could haul you up, earth, sea and all. Then I should make the rope fast to a pinnacle of Olympus, and leave everything to dangle in mid-air. By so much does my strength exceed the strength of gods and men."[4] Then, having recalled this great truth, he set out for Mount Ida to weigh the fate of the Achaeans and Trojans in his golden scales. He is an administrator of the cosmos, with many cares and considerable merit, but he is not Yahweh, the Creator of heaven

[4] *Iliad*, 8, 18–27. [Trans. E. V. Rieu, p. 145.]

and earth. R. Schaerer rightly considers this description of Zeus to be the finest illustration of Homeric wisdom and one of the keys to Greek religious thought.[5] Did they ever give it up? An answer is provided by another authority on Greek literature: "Even when it freed itself from all anthropomorphism, the typically Greek ideal of divinity clearly implies a personal god and not an impersonal force, and always leaves room for a number of other more or less completely divine beings, however inferior to the Supreme Being these may be. 'Exclusive' monotheism was never a Greek belief."[6] For the Greeks what was eternal was the cosmos, ἀνάγκη, μοῖρα. The general manager of the forces of the world was not an ultimate reality in the sense ascribed to him in the religion of the Old Testament.

Whatever the intellectual problems it has entailed, the theism that prevailed upon the human mind was that of the Old Testament, not that of Homer. It is a more difficult belief, but there is no longer any other God to whom we could agree to pray. If God has to face up to fate, this second part of our study would be pointless; prayer between human beings can easily be expanded into prayer to spirits or the demiurge without any radical transformation. Early Christian writers were conscious of the originality of their prayer and one of them even ventured to say that "no one is against God save God himself".[7] This assertion expresses the tragedy of existence and of prayer in a metaphysical maxim, debatable in some respects, but with an element that is inescapably true.

3. God Penetrates me Wholly

This is a third radical difference between divine and human prayer. It is true, as we have said, that at the peak of prayer between human beings, moments of perfect, though fleeting, mutuality may occur when the two involved in it entirely understand and give themselves

---

[5] R. Schaerer, *L'Homme antique et la structure du monde intérieur d'Homère à Socrate*, Paris, 1959, Conclusion.

[6] J. H. Rose in the collective work, *La Notion du divin depuis Homère jusqu'à Platon*, Geneva, 1954, p. 21.

[7] "*Nemo contra Deum nisi Deus.*" This is the theme of G. K. Chesterton's *The Man who was Thursday*.

to each other (at least in principle, for of course their respective beings are still incomplete and this mutual love is precisely the way to their completion). But the mutual relationship between God and man is something altogether different; God wants me wholly, God forestalls me, God knows me, and in the depths of my being is more truly myself than I am. He is simultaneously totally different from me, and my innermost reality. I cannot reverse these statements and say that I want God wholly, that I forestall him, etc.; at least, I can only do so secondarily, after he has addressed me, and even then such ideas would be inoperative without his aid. Any claim to beget God is an *a priori* absurdity, even though by an act of divine grace and an Incarnation, it can finally be vindicated—as a kind of startling paradox. The fact that I have a past and a future, that I first receive my being before I make any attempt to bestow being— herein lies the proof that my relations with God will always consist in a defective mutuality in which I shall be totally dependent.

Nothing of this kind binds me to a human being. Ordinarily among human beings there is mutual transcendence or independence, and exceptionally a mutual immanence. With regard to God's relationship to me, at every moment of my life, he is both transcendent and immanent, but I, for my part, cannot use either term with regard to my relationship to him. My movements are always in him and I cannot get beyond him, nor withdraw from him; and yet, I am always far from his centre, which I can neither possess nor make use of. Man is my neighbour, he is like myself; God is my originating principle, my absolute superior, who for ever escapes me, from whom I can never escape. Therefore, the prayer I address to God is already within him. The prayer I address to my fellow man is external to him, or, more accurately, the prayer that I address to him presupposes that each of us is, by nature, external to the other and that I am trying through prayer to bridge the gap that divides us. But the prayer that I address to God presupposes that, whether at the beginning or at the end, God is not outside me, but that I myself am outside him and external to him, although I am trying to make the distance less and less, like a curve conscious of its approach to its asymptote.

The two types of prayer have many things in common. But, if we may use another mathematical comparison, the relation which connects us with God is not in origin symmetrical; the Creator and the created being are not like two integral realities with a common potency, that could be included as univocal elements in a single system. When we say that God penetrates us wholly we mean that he is essentially and eternally prior to all our thoughts and desires. We are surrounded and known to the core, and this gives our prayers a characteristic which they never possess to the same degree and with the same constancy when their object is a fellow man.

The analyses we have just outlined suffice to show the insurmountable complexity of the idea of God for the human mind, which is completely outstripped and lost when faced with infinite Being. The attempt to work out the relations between men was sufficiently baffling. *A fortiori*, the attempt to work out our relationship with God is bound to be even more so. We have the hope—or the illusion —that we understand our own selves thoroughly when we keep to the realities within us and to our own domain. But when we turn to God neither the hope nor the illusion can be maintained. We cannot get to know God's being exhaustively, we cannot control him, or make ourselves his equals; we see at once that the human mind cannot attain a self-evident view of God and that there will always be a *complexio oppositorum* with regard to him. So long as we have only our own strength wherewith to overcome him, we are hiped like Jacob in his combat with the angel.

Kierkegaard realised the tragic nature of this situation. "True prayer", he considered, "is a struggle with God and man emerges victorious when God is the victor."[8] To be alone in face of God demands so terrible an effort that men most often withdraw from it and this explains why they need society to mask their real condition and as an escape from the combat. It was the thought of this that drew from Kierkegaard a moving and most profound remark: "O,

[8] S. Kierkegaard, *Prières et fragments sur la prière* (Extracts from his *Journal*), trans. from the Danish by P. H. Tisseau, Bazoges-en-Pareds, 1937, p. 95.

how rare it is to be able to say Amen wholeheartedly to a prayer."[9] At the same time, the purpose of the combat is not so much to overcome God as to overcome ourselves by allowing him to convince us that we are understood by him. It has nothing in common with that which we noted above in the case of prayer between men, where the first step is to secure the attention of another man, and the next, insistently to make a request to which he seemed deaf and utterly inattentive. But mutual collaboration between God and man begins in a totally different context, for in this case we have no need to force our presence upon a Being who is unaware of it and indifferent to what we are saying. Prayer to God implies that the kind of effort that is required to draw human attention, ends. Even naïve or superstitious people show by their actions that they realise this: they will upbraid the saints who have failed to grant the favours they requested, and will punish their statues, but it would never occur to them to treat God with the same too human familiarity.

4. *God is the Plenitude of Holiness and can only be Reached by Faith in Prayer*

Human perception opens a window in the mystery of being; it is a freewill offering that beings make to each other as a result of an inclination which they have not produced but received and which determines their mutual relations. The perception of God, however, cannot be of the same kind as earthly knowledge, and he owes no obedience to a pre-established order, uncaused by himself, that would make him, in relation to us, merely our companion in fate here below. Since he is not perceptible in this way, other ways must be found. On earth, these ways will be prayer or, what amounts to the same thing, faith: this is the only conceivable form our conscious intercourse with him can assume. It is so, first of all, in the general sense in which faith is an apt word for the special mode of knowledge that occurs when the object is itself a being that can know, i.e. when there is an encounter between two conscious beings, and not between a conscious being and some reality in which consciousness is

[9] Ibid., p. 48.

lacking.[10] Then, in a more special sense, faith animated by prayer is the only earthly way of normally approaching God, for he is a knowable reality endowed with intellect who, among all other such realities, is utterly unique; he is far too deeply in the secret of their structure simply to be of their structure. And if, even in the mutual relationship between human minds, reflexion—a secondary movement—proves altogether inadequate to the task, so that the vocative alone can establish contact and continuity between them, how much more must this be so, *a fortiori*, when it is God who is to be reached!

"Faith lives on prayer; indeed faith is, strictly speaking, nothing other than prayer. From the moment we begin truly to believe, we are already praying, and when prayer ends, faith ends also."[11] B. Häring, who quotes this idea of Emil Brunner's, goes so far as to maintain that both prayer and faith presuppose the beginning of a revelation. To pray to a God who is merely the logical conclusion of a process of human reasoning seems to him an absurdity. And if in reply I say that God has endowed me with reason precisely that I may come to the conclusion that he exists, this is the equivalent of saying that God has taken the first step, that God has revealed himself; and the author interprets in this sense Möhler's expression according to which the human reason is an organ for receiving information (*das vernehmende Organ*): "Reality is first laid hold of, only afterwards are the conclusions drawn."[12] The fact that we have to prove the existence of God, is, for Möhler, the not very reassuring sign that mankind has fallen; the fact that we *can* prove it is the sign that he naturally and generally reveals himself in us. The same line of thought occurs in Max Scheler who, seeing in the world a sign of

[10] I am using the word *faith* here in a very broad sense which does not go beyond the natural order, or at least need not. In the history of Western philosophy faith denotes: (1) opinion which does not reach certainty (Plato); (2) the intuition of the first principles of reasoning (Aristotle); (3) the knowledge of a knowable reality that is itself endowed with intellect, i.e. of a mind by another mind (some Neoplatonists). It is this third meaning which I make particularly my own. Cf. *Conscience et Logos*, pp. 183–5.

[11] B. Häring, *Das Heilige und das Gute*, Freiburg i. Br., 1950, pp. 33–49. "*Der Glaube lebt vom Beten, ja, der Glaube ist eigentlich nichts anderes als Beten. In dem Moment, wo wir wirklich glauben, beten wir schon, und wo das Beten aufhört, da hört auch der Glaube auf.*"

[12] "*Zuerst kommt das Vernehmen, dann erst das Schliessen*", ibid., p. 37.

God for the believer, links faith with dialogue, i.e. with a mode of knowledge which presupposes an interpersonal attitude, even if it takes the form of a question, on the part of the man who prays.[13]

Another way of demonstrating that prayer is really involved in mystery is to show that it is directed towards the supremely "holy" being. When we were dealing with prayer addressed to a created being, we observed that at its peak, it too enters a sacred zone. But the "holiness" of a creature is only the highest state of its own being, and it is an aspect of which it is summoned to become aware by a compelling call before it is able to ratify or explain it. But when God is in question, we at once observe very different characteristics: (1) It is his whole being that is holy and not only the root or the ideal future of his self-hood. As soon as I draw near him, I know that the secret of my being is about to be unveiled, because God is utterly unveiled to himself, utterly luminous, and he penetrates me through and through. (2) This aspect of totality coincides with an eternal act of his will; it is not an episode that he will experience earlier or later. (3) Unlike the "holy" which consists in the perfect development of the created being and is only the divine aspect of some particular creature; *a fortiori*, unlike the "holy" of disintegration which is demoniac; the "holiness" of God is the ground of the self-hood of all his subjects. Because of this, he *is* their holiness, and the origin of every definition of holiness, and indeed of every moral rule. He is, therefore, that form of holiness which is sanctity itself and the source of all sanctification.

It follows that there is an infinite distance between the created being who prays and his God. The mystery does not lie only in the divine mind which transcends my own, i.e. in the universal communicability of truth, and in the fact that, when I pray, I submit the resources of my own mind to a transcendent source; the mystery

---

[13] With regard to supernatural faith, the Council of Trent teaches that "dead faith" is possible. Is this also true of the less specific meaning of the word faith as used above? Is faith possible without love? No doubt it is, but not without some relationship with a previous or later love; and, in my case, it may be considered that there is no faith that is not in the vocative; a minimum vocative in the case of the indifferent sinner; a tragic vocative in the case of rebellion or repentance.

also lies in the divine holiness which sets me at a distance from it through its stark perfection. In a striking passage, a mystic, Mary of the Incarnation, declares: "It was shown to me that God is like a great sea, and that, just as the sea tolerates no impurity but casts it out, so this great sea of purity which is God will have nothing that is not pure, and casts out everything that smacks of death and impurity."[14] Our alienation from God also includes our alienation from ourselves and explains it. Without him, the internal dialogue we can have with ourselves would lack all mystery and lose most of its metaphysical interest. But the very statement of this fact is sufficient to prove that the distance of which we complain is not of the same kind as the disparity between two human beings who are strangers to each other. Neither God nor my being as it exists in him are strangers to me; God is not out of my range as a wall is outside the range of a bullet that fails to hit it; and I cannot say that prayer does not reach him or, if it reaches him, does not penetrate. Comparisons fail to express this relationship, and all of them more or less distort what we mean.

5. *God's Response has Nothing in Common with any Human Response*
What prayer between human beings and divine prayer have in common lies in the development of what we do, the indefinite progress that becomes possible to our action as a result of a mutual intercourse and a sustenance from which we benefit. The mere fact that we pray to God is no guarantee that we are rid of arid and illusory phrase-making, but a sincere prayer is a step towards its purification. It is not a static relationship, but a movement. There may well be a considerable admixture of error in the way we picture it, but this does not at all mean that in the subsequent idea the error is likely to be fatal.

How, it may be said, can we become aware of this purification? God's silence seems to deprive us of any means of checking the truth of what we say about him. However, the mind, on reflexion, does provide us with a control. I learn what he is through the changes

[14] Quoted by B. Häring and also by Penido, *La Conscience religieuse*, Paris, 1935, p. 225.

which I experience when I pray to him. William James, who denied that he was a mystic, compared himself to an iron bar that observes the magnetic field to which it is subjected by the effects of whatever stirs up its molecules. This is an important criterion, although it seems to be wholly indirect. Prayer is an action; it enables me to achieve my personal fulfilment and also to decipher the enigma of God by awakening me to the reality of his being.

In all this there is no radical difference between our encounter with God and that which we experience with our fellow men. Where the difference lies is in the fact that God's initiative is totally different from anything we could have imagined, so that his response may be an absolute surprise and even absolutely misconstrued. Would we not have to explode the world to be able to grasp that response? Our uncertainty springs from our tendency to shut our eyes, and from our impossibility, in our present state, of always avoiding idolatry. We hunger and thirst for God's presence, but we have an astounding ability to provide ourselves with erroneous substitutes for that presence. We grieve that we cannot find God and we begin our search by discarding him. We look for his signature in the events of life, but we define those events in a way that must exclude his signature. We describe the natural world in terms that make the divine transcendence a forgotten and forgetting power. Obviously if we consider the world to be entirely self-sufficient we shall consider God not to be self-sufficient, and if then we assert that he is, we become entangled in irreconcilable contradictions.

But it is not only in their content that the divine and human responses differ: it is also in their mode. The nearer we come to God the more we are surprised. His ways are not our ways. They adapt themselves to our ways in order to make contact with us, but in doing so they introduce an unceasing and ever-recurring paradox, e.g. in those trials which bring peace, or in those moments of peace which provoke disturbing problems. We have not begun to grasp the meaning of the life of religion if we do not immediately realise that in it the notions of presence and response have a meaning that is totally different from that which they possess in our ordinary experience.

A convenient and partially true escape from this difficulty is to limit the divine response to a constant drive to make us deny the worth of our present values. God answers us by giving us a spirit of dissatisfaction. It has been said that he manifests himself "as that radical impossibility for us of being at one with ourselves, as that distance between ourselves and all reality which provokes the endless succession of poetic images and the incantations of mystics and poets. God's great gift to us is our unlimited power of detachment. Prayer is undoubtedly an expression of our acceptance of this requirement and of this incentive—both from God. It allows God to effect our deliverance from that narrow possessiveness which hinders us from accepting the inter-relationship of the realities of the universe and from perceiving what they reveal".[15] The essential function of negation in our minds is to correct the errors of our private judgement: in us, therefore, it is the delegate of other human minds, and in them all, the delegate of God. Hence God's answer to our prayers is a way of making us understand the meaning of his negations so that we may thereby transcend ourselves.

Nevertheless, we cannot confine God's utterances to this negative aspect, even when tempered by symbols. J. Trouillard remarks very aptly: "Symbolism is the sign that thought always awakens too late."[16] And yet, must we always think of human thought as a failure? May it not be a form of communion with God? There is no *a priori* reason to deny that God's response may be given through the most varied modes of our experience, including those of the senses; and God would not be God if he could not manifest himself positively in our minds. An excessive emphasis on the spirit of negation may *also* lead to our reducing the irreducible, and horribly curtailing the scope of divine activity. In actual fact, believers have always held that God's response comes sometimes as a particular

[15] J. Trouillard, "Symbole et distance", in *Le Symbole*, cahier 29 of *Recherches et débats* (Dec. 1959), p. 42. An English author, T. R. Miles, *Religion and the Scientific Outlook*, London, 1959, also agrees that God should be heard in silence with the aid of parables, and in these he would substitute generous self-abandonment ("commitment and dedication") for petition.

[16] J. Trouillard, op. cit., p. 43. The whole of this fine article deserves close attention.

happening, sometimes as the meaning of all particular happenings whatever they may be. But these last two varieties do not differ so much as might at first be imagined, for an event is nothing apart from what it signifies, and its religious "significance" is nothing if it does not inwardly modify the natural boundaries of the event. Certainly the sign of this sign is the negation, but the response from on high gives us a taste of its quality before it is analysed as a contrast or negation.

This is why the true significance of God's response is eminently positive. It keeps us from somnolence; it stirs us to be always moving forward; its pace is so rapid that we think we are lost because we are outdistanced, but it begins and ends by catching up with us. In fact it is our only hope of catching up with ourselves and of *being* truly ourselves through its presence. That presence is not a mere negation; it is our home ground and our resting place. It brings a message that differs from any created reality, for God is the Unique. He gives meaning to everything else, not by sterilising our being, but by arousing our activity and making us choose the way we shall go.

CHAPTER 2

The Psychological Stages of Prayer

We shall now try to classify the stages of prayer using the ancient adage of spiritual writers: *ab exterioribus ad interiora, ab interioribus ad superiora*. It has been handed down from Neoplatonism; in some respects it is inadequate,[1] and yet it would be rashness to deny that it is a summary of universal experience. A man of God is not necessarily a hermit hidden away in a geographical desert;[2] but he does need to withdraw from the world and find his God in some kind of silence.

It is difficult to cover the stages of prayer without mentioning its modes, i.e. without enquiring whether it should be individual or corporate, silent or vocal, etc. But at this point we shall discuss these matters as little as possible, because we shall give them due attention in a later chapter when we come to deal with the liturgy.

1. *Ab exterioribus ad interiora*

The first stage of prayer addressed to God would appear to be centripetal. We withdraw into ourselves. Recollection, silence, solitude: such is the teaching of the spiritual writers, and, in particular, of the *Imitation of Jesus Christ*. Consider some of its famous passages: "Whoever is resolved to live an inward and spiritual life must, with

[1] St Augustine quotes it with a variation: "*Revocat se [anima] ab exterioribus ad interiora, ab inferioribus ad superiora et dicit: Lauda anima mea Dominum.*" *Enarrationes in Ps.* 145, 5; PL, 37, 1887.

[2] The studies of Fr Sainsaulieu show that life in the desert is not so conducive to recollection as might be imagined: it abounds in material worries, it carries the risk of endless dangers, it disturbs the imagination and easily upsets the balance of the mind. The story of the hermits is exciting and complex, but, in any case, the symbol of the desert is inseparable from the history of prayer. Cf. the article by Fr Sainsaulieu, "Érémitisme" in the *Dictionnaire d'Histoire et de Géographie ecclésiastiques*.

Jesus, withdraw from the crowd."[3] The inner life is a life lived within oneself; and "the man of inner life easily recollects himself, since he is never wholly immersed in outward affairs".[4] It is the central thesis of the whole book that "truth speaks in the inner man without the noise of words",[5] and that compunction of heart is incompatible with the dissipation of the senses.

Madame Guyon gives a striking account of this returning movement into the self: "As soon as the soul is sloping towards its own centre, i.e. has withdrawn into itself by recollection, then, in that instant, it becomes immensely active and sweeps towards its centre with a rapidity incomparably greater than any other action."[6] Even in the life of the body reflex action is astonishingly prompt, but it seems that when the spirit withdraws into itself the introversion is faster and goes deeper; consider the philosopher (Descartes) shutting himself up in his stove or a devout man preparing himself for prayer.

Recollection signifies two things: a turning away from external phenomena, and the pacification within our souls of the tumult produced by the imagination and the emotions, so that concentration may be certain. But it is not easy to establish this silence and to do so instantly. It may be a physical impossibility to go into one's inner room and shut the door upon oneself, but even so this is not our most troublesome task. If we are to quell the thronging commotion within us we need both eagerness and method. Eagerness alone (of the kind suggested by the passage from Madame Guyon and observable in the *raptus* of the mystics) may often lead to a disorganised and unbalanced life of the spirit; method alone (of the type indicated in the *Spiritual Exercises* of St Ignatius, in which even the rhythm of the subject's breathing is controlled) may well lead us no further than the stage of meditation.

Not a result to be sniffed at, it may be said! And, of course, meditation is a profitable, and, indeed, indispensable step forward. Its

[3] *The Imitation of Christ*, 1, 20, 8. [Trans. L. Sherley-Price, Penguin Books, p. 50.]
[4] Ibid., 2, 1, 35, p. 69.
[5] Ibid., 3, 2.
[6] Quoted by J. Chansou, *La Prière*, Toulouse, 1927, p. 14.

meaning, however, has been the subject of differing interpretations. St Thomas, for example, keeping to the age-old monastic tradition, considers it to be an exercise that follows on *lectio* and consists essentially in listening to God's word in the Scriptures. It thus precedes *oratio*, the act of speaking to God. It has, therefore, an intermediary function. Suarez, on the other hand, in the sixteenth century, held a rather different view: "*Studiosa mentis actio occultae veritatis notitiam ductu propriae rationis investigans.*" The setting has altered and meditation has become an almost independent activity. In the *Treatise on the Love of God* (6, Chap. 2) by St Francis de Sales, it is called "the first degree of prayer, or mystical theology".

At the present day it is the Suarezian definition that is generally accepted. Meditation is made up of "points"; its aim is to tranquillise the inner life and to strengthen it; it builds up the self through the analysis of an idea and the education of our faculty of attention. It is a remarkable fact that with regard to this first phase of initiation into the spiritual life the spiritual writers in no way condemn the self; they tell us to withdraw into ourselves, and yet at other times they say we should get rid of or despise the self. In the *Imitation*, even within the limits of a single chapter, the change in tone is startling. Compare, for example, Book 1, Chap. 1, 5: "Look for an opportunity to be concerned with yourself", and Chap. 2, 25: "A true understanding and humble estimate of oneself is the highest and most valuable of all lessons"; and yet earlier in this second chapter the "conceited intellectual who knows the courses of the stars" is reproached because he "neglects his own soul"!

Withdrawal from the world, withdrawal from one's personal fantasies, this means that by a twofold renunciation we free ourselves from the spell of the world of nature and make ourselves ready and disposed for an act of inner attention. Malebranche seems to have held that this was enough, since he defines prayer as an act of attention on the part of the soul. And yet so far nothing has even as much as begun. For to what are we supposed to pay attention? To ourself? We have just seen that the ego is equivocal, and provides a problem rather than a solution. Prayer cannot be content with this. It requires silence, but it is not a narcissistic recollection. It is a form of expectation; it means that we have put ourselves at God's service; it is an invocation—to use the expressions of Gabriel Marcel. If this were not so, then the attitude of a philosopher in his meditations would be identical with that of the religious man in his prayer, and this is untrue.

In fact there may be a very real difference between recollection and prayer in the strict sense. When Marcel Proust took refuge in his soul and found there the memory of times past, when Sâmkhya leads us into that innermost self which is above and beyond this changing world,[7] can we say that this is prayer in the theistic sense which we have accepted? It is debatable. But a very definite answer was supplied by the president of the Third International Buddhist Congress, some years ago: "We must rid the world of the idea of God which only serves to foster the totalitarian outlook. Let us not waste our time in saying prayers which are quite useless. . . . Meditation and the concentration of millions of individual minds aiming at peace is the only way to obtain it and to maintain it in the world."[8] For this point of view, meditation becomes the essential form of devotion, the only form worth preserving as the legacy of the historical religions.

The practical conclusion from all this will be either a judicious meditation on the world, or a critical survey of intentions or memories with a view to adding depth to our inner life.

We should, however, be very careful never to scorn the practice and technique of recollection. For these constitute the last obstacle to irreligion, the last moment before religion departs. As long as meditation persists, the hope for the continuance of prayer on earth remains.

The practice of recollection means that we are on the alert for some absolute truth and reality in the innermost depth of our being. But who can say, a priori, what he is going to find in that depth? Recollection of any kind, opens the windows of the soul. Once this has been done, something decisive has been achieved; once opened they will never close again hermetically.

[7] R. C. Zaehner, At Sundry Times, London, 1958, pp. 45–8.
[8] Quoted in L'Actualité religieuse, 15 March 1955.

2. *Ab interioribus ad superiora*

In this second stage, the initial forms of prayer are not lost but integrated. Meditation and inner concentration, at least in their form that is traditional in the West, have not been practised *in vacuo*; they have indeed meant a withdrawal from the world, but at the same time a systematic review of ideas. This purposive structure links up with states or acts of the soul that open up to a Being other than ourselves. In contemplative prayer, as it was practised, for instance, by the French schools of the seventeenth century, the purpose was to pray to God, but not anarchically. Prayer was systematic, balanced; a method gave a structure to spontaneous impulse. Even today, at Saint-Sulpice, the exercise lasts for three-quarters of an hour (one quarter kneeling, one quarter sitting, one quarter standing); silence alternates with speech; a definite theme is proposed, but there is freedom in dealing with it. This arrangement is considered to be fundamental and mental prayer understood in this way is taken to be the root of all prayer, or at least, it is the lever that sets it in motion every morning. It finds room for all the faculties and requires them all to contribute to this calling upon God.

What precisely does the soul's movement towards transcendence consist in? First, let us note the elements to which it cannot be reduced. It is not a mere movement of aspiration. J. Segond, in his study of prayer, gives aspiration a place of extreme importance and a character of deliberate vagueness. According to him, the essence of prayer is to connect us with an "inexhaustible source of personal autonomy and universal charity", and he refuses any further definition of its nature. Consequently, on this view, the best definition of the spiritual life is the raising up of the mind and intellect. "The kingdom of God consists of the inner man coming to an awareness of himself." Segond, in short, gives his approval to these words of Diderot: "O God, I do not know whether you exist, but I shall direct my thoughts as if you were seeing right into my soul, and I shall act as if I were in your presence."[9] These are words to which, it would seem, the Newman of the *Apologia* would have been strongly opposed: "If this were to be allowed [Newman is referring to deduc-

9 J. Segond, *La Prière*, Paris, 1925, pp. 2, 51, etc.

tions from Butler's theory that all truth is only probable], then the
celebrated saying, 'O God, if there be a God, save my soul, if I have
a soul!' would be the highest measure of devotion:—but who can
really pray to a Being, about whose existence he is seriously in
doubt?"[10] The sensitive and sorrowful mind of J. Segond certainly
makes manifest the implicit and obscure elements which prayer involves, at least for some persons who are acutely aware of their own
inadequacy and of the mystery of things. Nevertheless, it is obvious
that the movement of prayer would entail a contradiction if, being
theistic in form, the end to which it addresses itself were not so.
Newman gave the psychological movement a logical direction. To
surrender to Nature, to take refuge in the subconscious, or even to
strive to reach the higher level of the ideal self in supplication, however noble—none of this really meets the demand of the *ad superiora*
element of prayer. For St Thomas this involves an *ascensus intellectus
in Deum*, and at the very least God's shadow should be perceptible
as covering the realities to which we ascend in prayer.

However, this approach of the soul to God can assume a number
of forms. The simplest of these seems to be that of a conversation
with God. In fact this seems to be the most common way in which
prayer is understood. A. Fonck notes that the Fathers held three
ideas about this: a request made to God, a conversation with God,
or a raising of the soul to him. He considers the second to be the
best, and yet he also quotes a passage from Bellarmine in which this
idea of a "dialogue" with God is considerably soft-pedalled.
Bellarmine certainly does not consider as a perfection the state in
which we speak to God without knowing whether we have been
heard, or even the state in which, though reasonably assured that
we are being heard, we have no clear answer. But he says that the
highest stage of prayer is like a human conversation, but is also
different, inasmuch as the soul in prayer listens far more than it
speaks. It receives enlightenment; unwearyingly and never allowing
itself to be distracted, it concentrates on prayer, listening and keeping quiet.[11]

[10] J. H. Newman, *Apologia pro vita sua*, London, 1890, p. 19.
[11] *Dictionnaire de Théologie catholique*, article "Prière", col. 175.

A too human idea of conversation with God leads to obvious absurdities. The chatterbox transfers his wordy self-satisfaction, more or less innocently, into his spiritual life. He is always talking about himself and never listens; he pesters God with his appeals as though God were deaf and needed waking up.[12] Carried to an extreme this means the end of authentic prayer; it becomes a diarrhoea of religious verbosity, a linguistic intemperance akin to the habit of speaking to oneself with which some people are afflicted. A close relative of the chatterbox is the mythomaniac who supplies both the questions and their answers; he imagines that he is listening, but in reality he listens to nothing at all. Self-exuberance receives back its own echo. Its dialectic is purely subjective; it is smothering and undisciplined.

Fortunately, however, besides these degenerate forms, there are others which constitute a definitely religious dialogue. Once we realise that God is the absolute we shall try to expose our minds to his influence. Neither the questions nor the answers will be of the same brand as those used in human intercourse. They may be analogous, they will not be replicas. For, by definition, God is utterly our superior; he is the Being that no name can encompass; he cannot be truly called "thou", or "I" or "he" or "we". It is, therefore, impossible to avoid the fact that between his questions and ours, our answers and his, there is a profound qualitative difference. Not that he questions less or answers less, but that we are unable, from our own resources, to enter into the divine circuit, because our mouths and ears are clogged.

No organ of ours can contain him, and when he draws us to himself he speaks through every fibre of our being. He is not far from us. St Paul says that it is "in him we live and move and have our being", but we do not possess any special faculty or sense wherewith to reach him, in the way we reach the realities of nature. It is true that from Origen to St Bonaventure the theory of the "spiritual senses" had its adherents and provoked speculation. But when such speculation is closely scrutinised it turns out to be a matter of

---

[12] St Gregory has an amusing expression on this point: "*Orare est amaros gemitus in compunctione resonare*" (ibid.).

metaphors or else to refer to momentary transformations of our ordinary means of information. There is never any question of a sixth sense or of an intuition introduced like an extra faculty from outside. It is with our whole being that we are religious, and not by means of some supplementary organ specifically reserved for religion.[13]

If we would understand the communication involved in authentic prayer we must turn to the analogies provided by the highest moments of our experience, realising, of course, that in order to be applied to God, all of them require to be transformed, although not one of them is too low to reflect the mystery of his being. It is often said that the silent concord of human love images the love of God. When two human beings are united in a perfect mutual relationship, words cease to be necessary, and may even be obstructions: in silence they are more completely immanent to each other than if words intervened restricting their intercourse to a merely partial communication. This is true. But in this case silence becomes a language, and, in the circumstances, a more efficient and positive language than speech. Its value does not arise from absence of content or negation, but from the previously accumulated wealth, now noiselessly given, without any distracting commotion, given in an unalterable and joyful plenitude. It is this hidden wealth that matters, and we can perceive a rich silence of this kind underlying some kinds even of spoken conversation. In art, for instance, we occasionally receive some such revelation. There are songs without words that nevertheless speak, there are pictures that convey a message with a gracious and sacred authority, works of poetry and prose that through the outward mechanism of their phrases make visible another world than ours.

All this helps us to understand that prayer is a dialogue with God, although it cannot be reduced to the pattern of our human conversations with their conventionality and shallowness. It is a dialogue that never descends to a mediocre level, and that is why it troubles the human mediocrities that we are. We take chatter to be the

[13] I gain this impression from the issue of *Études carmélitaines* devoted to the question "Nos sens et Dieu", Paris, 1954, and especially from the article by M. Olphe-Galliard, pp. 179–93.

expression of reality, and so we tend to feel that on the mountain peaks of God there is nothing we can find, whereas in fact it is there that everything begins all over again. Prayer directed to God is directed to contemplation and ecstasy. It wrenches us from our little privet-hedges and our isolation. It is an expression of our being, or an offering of that being which, even when we are weary, means that we are being taken over by God. Prayer means that we have an "appetite" for God, and therefore we cannot be content with the humdrum horizon of our "normal" selves; we cease to consider the area within our garden fence as the centre of the universe; we even forget that we are praying because we are intent on homing towards the being who is its end.

From a different point of view, however, we can see that we out-distance our own level only because another pulls us out from it and delivers us, in such a way that we can adapt ourselves to his presence always above and beyond our attainment. Thus God questions quite as much as he answers us; he only answers us and only moves us to question him or answer him after he has first questioned us himself. Prayer is certainly a dialogue; it is an ascending dialogue which always makes use of language, but is enslaved to no particular language, and often dispenses with verbal answers. This independence, this acceleration in the speed of intercourse, this ascending dialogue, tend to make us consider that it is no longer a dialogue. Philosophers, naturally enough, are inclined to regard it as, simply, contemplation.[14] Popular instinct, on the other hand, in spite of its obvious shortcomings, happily avoids this reduction in the status of religion; and philosophers who would wish to impose it, would be putting an end to a uniquely valuable resource of religion.

We are going to maintain that spiritual recollection is only the first stage in prayer and that the transition from the inner life to a

[14] It is this view that accounts for P. Guérin's remark that prayer was "unknown to the wisdom of the Greeks except as contemplation. It hardly occurs in Plato and was quite unknown to Aristotle. For them the highest spirituality was intelligence, the grasp of reality which we gain through understanding it, nothing more." *Vérité et Religion*, Paris, 1962, p. 178. This is a hard saying. We have Socrates' prayers for purity of soul. The Stoic Cleanthes, in his hymn to Zeus, even intercedes for sinners and asks God to enlighten them. And there is a Neoplatonic spirituality which does not restrict itself to Plotinian contemplation.

life beyond and above it, far from destroying the essential mutuality of prayer, is in reality a staggering increase of it, a breathless acceleration. Moreover, the soul's relationship with God is situated in time and although it is engaged in eternity, prayer involves a developing process. What is true, is that the process is hidden from spectators who are merely curious. Such spectators we ourselves become when we laboriously exhibit the episodes of our interior life. For these concern only ourselves and our Creator. Pascal was right when he left the notes about it in his *Mémorial* in cipher; for sometimes the only way to explain what has happened without distortion, is enigmatic utterance.[15]

Does this mean that we abandon all idea of verification? Not in the least. In fact we have two means for this. One of them is immediate: the novelty of the message which the soul feels it has received and which gives it a spiritual push forward.[16] The other is more widespread and covers our being as a whole, and especially our moral standards; it shows us whether our first impression really had the significance we imagined. The first criterion is only an approximation, it can never suffice; the second adds a life-time's coherence to the promise of an instant: thought is added to intuition. The progress of the spiritual life cannot dispense with wisdom; into the journey of our private lives it brings a potential universality.

Nevertheless, verification lands us with a responsibility which we cannot shift to others. Another man may advise us; he cannot be

[15] I do not intend to decide the question, but simply to point out the problem of the possibility of the soul's self-expression. In an admirable book on *L'Amour et la mort*, Paris, 1959, G. Gargam takes the view that since the infinite is inaccessible and inexpressible, "death intervenes as a necessity" (p. 17) whenever the soul tries to reach or communicate the infinite, as happens in love. But C. Le Chevalier, *La Confidence et la personne humaine*, Paris, 1960, appears to hold that the soul's infinity, or the infinity within the soul, can be followed all along its winding way and be wholly conveyed in words, provided that these remain restrained; paradoxically, everything can be transmitted so long as it remains implicit. Although the main subject of these two works is not prayer, their contrasting attitude is very relevant to the problem of prayer.

[16] P. Guérin gives this subtle and profound example: "Forgiveness is deserved only if we do not forgive ourselves. Here precisely it becomes evident that prayer is answered." For, if through prayer we feel that we are the more pardoned for pardoning ourselves the less, then the answer is radically distinct from any auto-suggestion: "A new kind of existence, beyond the human, comes into being." *Vérité et Religion*, pp. 185–6.

our substitute. In religion we must accept a personalism analogous to that of Aristotle in ethics when he says that it is the wise man who, in the last resort, decides what Virtue is. Even when we have consulted others, the final decision is our own; we ourselves have to get rid of illusions, and acquire wisdom and gradually implant it in our murky hearts. All things must be made of use to us; the spirit of criticism, of judgement, cannot be separated from the authentically mystical spirit; therefore, *a fortiori*, and even more extensively, it cannot be separated from the authentically religious spirit. It is precisely because there is no special faculty for approaching God, for speaking to him and hearing him, that no faculty is out of place in the practice of religion or in the organisation of prayer. Sensation is no less useful than thought, and thought is no less useful than feeling. The significant act of our calling upon God must preserve every one of the elements that go to make up our spontaneous life, and, then too, those that belong to the life of recollection. But it uses in a new direction the elements it integrates; and the control exercised over prayer is itself a final element in prayer, a discipline contained in, not imposed on, revelation.

3. The Return to the Outside World

Since prayer is a dialogue it is not the mind's fleeing far away from itself. Neither is it a flight from the world. It gives the created being a new direction, but it does not withdraw from it. That is why the Neoplatonic formula is neither complete nor altogether correct. "From without to within; then from within to the regions above." We agree; and yet the man who prays to God does not vanish in the clouds like Elijah; he remains here, and, in a sense, more concentrated than ever on the world he was supposed to have forgotten. He has not so much left it as turned a new gaze on it so that he now lives in it from within his and its source in God.

Man is so situated that he learns things successively and moves forward by stages in a reality which, after all, is an indivisible whole. Therefore, we must respect the educational development of prayer; after the withdrawal into the self there follows the movement in transcendence. But should we not add a third stage, which is a return to the outside world?

This idea could obviously be equivocal, but with this possibility eliminated, it was acceptable even to St John of the Cross as a promise dependent upon the gift of grace.[17] Dissipation makes us strangers to ourselves, and yet the upward flight of prayer can also effect an estrangement. Failure to perceive this would lead to grievous errors. In all human activity there is a risk of both a double meaning and a perversion of meaning. The possibility of more than one meaning is a proof that we do not possess reality in its fullness, but it is also a sign that we are meant to reach that fullness, and that it is a living reality traversed by currents of consciousness. Were it not so, there could be no genuine personal activity and no genuine prayer.

In modern times the classical expression of the stages of prayer has seldom been criticised by spiritual writers. In many cases, however, an equivocal element has insinuated itself into its interpretation. For we find an increasing tendency to see in the *interiora*, not ourselves or a world of inner realities, but the deepest meaning of the *exteriora*, i.e. the inner meaning of the events and beings that surround us, their ultimate purpose as willed by God. Thus the *superiora* and the *interiora* of the classical expression have been transferred to external reality. This extraversion of prayer and this spiritual concern for God's purpose in the world have always been present in Christian prayer in spite of the Neoplatonic nature of its external form. In our time, however, this presence has become resistance; with great conviction we maintain and exalt the value of created beings; we cannot accept that they should be in any way violated or depreciated. Of course, the vision of their magnitude in God, is valid; at the same time this assessment of their value contains a danger of atheism and could imply the virtual liquidation of divine prayer.

These remarks show that the notion of "signification" is itself equivocal. The *meaning* of a thing may be my intended action upon it, or the action of some other person. Who is this other? If it is an

[17] "Nos Sens et Dieu", pp. 194–212.

object which is itself capable of subjective action (if, for example, it is some other person), the meaning of its being may depend upon itself or upon some third object or person, but if it is merely a material object, such multiplication cannot occur; the material object does not give itself a meaning, it receives it from the world of conscious subjects. But above all such human subjects there is the Creator. If we would have a religious understanding of created beings, must we not pray to God for enlightenment about them? And is not respect for their objective natural reality the preliminary condition for this prayer? To understand events or even persons we must first discover their structure and their inherent tendency, quite independently of any private intention we may have of imposing modifications on them. This shows the complexity of religious *meaning*, and how, in a very definite way, it encourages scientific observation. Prayer demands accuracy before it begins, that robust realism which does not constitute religion, but without which religion would be questionable indeed. The scientist's impartiality makes contact with an initial strand of a being's existence as it is willed by the Creator, that which corresponds to its insertion in the world of sense; the impartiality of the religious view of things should be inspired by the same spirit and continue it, but it should go beyond the conditions whereby things exist together in nature, and penetrate beneath their outer surface to the core that contains their more intimate constructive and purposive reality.

One of the more valuable intuitions of Fr Teilhard de Chardin undoubtedly seems to be this restoration to natural science from within of a religious orientation, the search for the intrinsic meaning in the movement of things. It makes the world an altar whereon the sacrifice of the man who prays can be offered; in fact he himself becomes an offering whose prayer is that he has at last become conscious of his meaning. God's purpose is not just my desire or my ambition, however universal; it must be that which created being contains in its heart through the will of the Creator. How can I know what this is if I do not begin by accepting and observing phenomena? Outward reality can thus help to purify inward perception; it can be of service in our journey to the *superiora*, not only because it is there that the soul must act and find the touchstone of its self-giving, but also because it compels devotion to regard the universe with respect, and because it condemns beforehand any attempts on our part to control it or to fly from it, however well-intentioned they may be. This return to the *exteriora* does not bring about any divorce between them and the *superiora*; the *interiora* join both together because they show at one and the same time the meaning of our prayer and that of being. As we mount up, through the world to God, we hasten towards our meeting with the God who reveals himself at the heart of the world and of the world's history as an inexhaustible force of new life or of correction.

CHAPTER 3
The Ends of Prayer

1. *The Traditional Divisions*

The ends to which prayer is ordained are very clearly enumerated in a quotation from an eminent spiritual writer and humanist, Fr Grou, which is given in the *Dictionnaire de Théologie catholique*: "Prayer, like sacrifice, deals with four things: adoration, thanksgiving, forgiveness of sin, procuring of spiritual and temporal benefits. The first two are in direct relationship with God and are therefore unquestionably the most important. The last two are related to our own concerns which are subordinate to those of God and which we should only envisage after his."[1] This division based on the theology of the four ends of sacrifice has found its way into the catechism and is familiar to all Catholics.

Some authors, however, do not think it adequate, and A. Fonck, for example, in the article we have just mentioned, suggests a seven-fold classification: adoration, praise, thanksgiving, contrition, love, self-abandonment, petition. These changes are not very adventurous, but at least they indicate that the phenomenology of prayer is still obscure. Mediaeval spiritual writers had gone much further in their investigations, but some theologians seem to have forgotten this. In no chapter of the psychology of the higher mental states has there reigned an anarchy like this, no less complete for being masked by the comforting analysis we quoted above.

An entire book would be required if we were to reach some real—as opposed to merely apparent—clarity on this subject. We must content ourselves with pointing out some omissions from the classical list that are extremely serious.

(1) The prayer of offering has no real place in any of the four

[1] Article, "Prière", by A. Fonck, col. 181.

categories put forward, and yet it is at the heart of all spirituality. By offering I mean a movement of the soul which is very different from adoration in the strict sense, and which consists in making of oneself a gift to God, in entering on his service. St Thomas called this act, an inward act, *devotio*. In our time we should call it love expressed in self-offering. It can be of varying degrees, and its perfect form would be the putting of ourselves at God's disposal in the way that a nun, a novice mistress, advised Margaret Mary: "Now go and present yourself to God, as a canvas before its painter."[2] To put the matter very simply, this prayer of offering consists in presenting oneself and the world to God, in such a way that the realm of created beings, in spite of everything that afflicts it, is subjected to God and becomes holy, cooperating in the movement which originates in him. A young displaced person, a convert, J. Lévy, expressed this movingly in a letter which Gabriel Marcel has published: "I look at myself as I appear to myself to be: a sickly chap, full of fancies; I mean to do good, but lack the energy to fight for it. My body is weak, my intellect (that intellect of which I am so proud) much enfeebled, my character worn out. What am I really good for? My professional worth as a philosophical student is extremely little: I am miles behind my fellows in formal knowledge, in ability to speak and produce an orderly discourse, in the authority that is required to direct a class of students. . . . And yet, I realise that this poor stuff which is me will become worthwhile if I make an offering of it. In fact it has already become so, since there are beings to whom I bring some strength. And yet, O my flesh, take no glory from this; my only desire is to be a servant."[3] It is through this self-offering that the prayer of those reduced to inactivity or close to death is seen to be so different from any imaginary reassertion of its claims on the part of the will to power. It is not a mystical exaltation of the self, but a renunciation of any personal claims, the admission that personally one can do nothing, and the costing gift of that nothingness to which we dearly cling. It is curious that so

---

[2] J. Segond, *La Prière*, Paris, 1925, p. 3.
[3] G. Marcel, *L'Homme problématique*, Paris, 1955, pp. 75–6.

fundamental an act should be missing from the classical list, or can only be included in it with the aid of sophisticated arguments.

(2) Similar remarks apply to another essential disposition—the desire for union with God. It might be called a form of adoration, and yet adoration is not specifically what the mystics call "adherence". On the contrary, it sets a distance between God and ourselves; we bow down in awe before his splendour, we acknowledge his transcendence; we do not necessarily feel the need to contemplate his face, we do not make explicit the adventurous wish to be united to him.

Can this desire for union with God be considered as included in the prayer of petition? At first sight this seems a sound idea and it fits in with the definition repeated so often down the ages: *petitio decentium a Deo*. Indeed the relationship between the two is profound, for all prayer is in a sense a form of petition, and this is a petition for the divine Spirit. But though petition is all inclusive, within its single genus many different species need to be distinguished. How is it possible not to give a special and outstanding place to the desire that God's presence may manifest itself, that his kingdom may come in us and in all men? This also may be truly called a strange omission. How is it that this purpose of prayer which has moved so many holy men to cry: "You, only you are my desire, O Lord", has failed to gain explicit recognition?

(3) In the preceding chapter we saw that the goal of prayer is the contemplation of God and the resulting dialogue with him. A spiritual man never wearies of that inner life of friendship that finds expression in unending intercourse with God and in the constantly renewed development of his being which results from the divine questioning of him and listening to him. For such a man the end of prayer is prayer, the situation in which God's self-manifestation stirs up the living answer of the human will. It is hardly credible that the love of God (in its twofold form, our love of him and his love of us) should not appear in the usual lists of the ends to which prayer looks. Of course, love is implied in the four ends normally given, but it is not explicit in the actual terms of any one of them. Thanksgiving is the one end that can most often be equated with the

loving will and with the desire to continue prayer as a paradise of unselfish mutuality. But even thanksgiving can conceal flattery or become degraded to mere conventionality.[4] *A fortiori*, the other three ends are also liable to be corrupted. It is difficult to see why that which should be the culmination of every spiritual act, the goal under which all other goals are subsumed, has not been high-lighted. Why should we not proclaim that *agape* is the ultimate conclusion of all four ends? Some pagan religions realised this. This is surprising enough when we consider their stage of development and remember the fact that in so many Christian books it is omitted. It becomes a scandal when we recall that Christianity is specifically the religion of *agape*, in which the theocentric reality is that to which all else is directed.

Fundamentally there is no other ultimate end to prayer than the love of God, i.e. a man's love for God in the hope of his love for man or in the rapture of experiencing it. Its subjective end is subordinate to an objective end, or, better, to an intersubjective end, which leaves God with absolute priority. This finality of prayer is probably only glimpsed in most religions; in their history it is an irregular phenomenon, and raises theological problems with which we are not now concerned.[5] But when it comes out into the open, it illuminates all other phenomena, and it can be seen that it is not only the ultimate purpose of prayer; it also gives prayer its form, and

[4] The history of religions affords more than one example of this. Among the Romans, thanksgivings offered publicly to the gods developed into solemnities organised for the glory of the generals. This development has been admirably studied by Léon E. Halkin, *La Supplication d'action de grâces chez les Romains*, Paris, 1953.

[5] Anyone interested in references to this matter should consult T. Ohm, *Die Liebe zu Gott in den nichtchristlichen Religionen*, Krailling vor München, 1950. The theological problem moved J. Maritain to write a very penetrating article in the *Études carmélitaines* on the "Nuit mystique" (esp. p. 137). Maritain suggests a notion of some sort of "atypical" supernatural which would enable us to explain God's action in elevating certain non-Christian souls, without denying that their mysticism remains halting and without a normal means of expression, in spite of the loving appeal which it contains. I should express his ideas in a different way and say that divine love raises man to a supernatural knowledge and love of God by making him retrace in obscurity the path that leads from ideas to persons, from the divine attributes to the living source where they originate, although no regular and explicit revelation of the Trinity to which he is really groping his way is made manifest.

from it we may proceed to consider all the forms which prayer assumes.

2. The Ends of Prayer and the Forms of Prayer

Love is the end of prayer and the origin of its forms. We shall illus- ✗ trate this by taking some examples of the typology of prayer from modern writers. We shall see, however, that these forms never monopolise the essence of prayer; not one of them is completely adequate to God's *agape*, or even to the *agape* which flows back from us to God. The position is similar to that which concerns God's attributes: no one of them adequately conveys his being and yet in each of them the living God expresses something of himself. Our prayer, like our thought, breaks up the divine unity; owing to our complex and inadequate natures we cannot receive his utter simplicity. And this is the reason why, in spite of the corrections we may make to the traditional list of the ends of prayer, we shall never be able to express the love which should animate it, in a perfectly adequate series of forms or types. We have to be content with approximations.

Such an approximation may be found in a little Anglican book, published at the end of the nineteenth century, and edited by two distinguished theologians, W. H. Frere and A. L. Illingworth.[6] It is an anthology of passages by Christian authors, grouped under two headings: intercession and thanksgiving. In a penetrating introduction, W. H. Frere gives his reasons for selecting these two forms. The first is directly related to charity towards our neighbour, the second to charity towards God. We will examine this more closely. Intercession appears to the author to be essential for any genuine advance in civilisation. Restless activity is a mere dispersal of energy even when it is the occasion of our meeting other people, but intercessory prayer produces contact with others; it widens our horizon and our sympathies; it can be co-extensive with all time and all space; it can join immensity with minuteness: for if we desire it, we

---

[6] *Sursum Corda*. A Handbook of Intercession and Thanksgiving, arranged by W. H. Frere and A. L. Illingworth, London & Oxford, 1898; small edition, 1905; reprinted 1958.

can enter into fellowship with the whole of creation, and, at the same time, it includes the humblest aspects of an individual being. "Things look their best and hopefullest when a man has prayed over them; the characters which are so discouraging and baffling are lit up with a new gleam of unsuspected possibilities."[7] Prayer creates or discovers a shining vocation in created beings; it does not merely exalt the man who is praying, it also illuminates those for whom he is interceding. It drives anxiety from the soul; it is the sovereign remedy for selfishness; it renews the face of the earth.

Now, between intercession and thanksgiving there is a close connexion. Gratitude to God is obviously a normal and easy expression of our love for him and springs from the love he shows to the beings he has created. But Bishop Frere does not stress this idea; he emphasises rather the advantages of thanksgiving; he sees it as the antidote to despondency, just as intercession is the antidote to selfishness. On this earth there are many reasons why we should feel cast down: the more legitimate of these reasons result from a consideration of our own faults; the others arise from the tragic events of human life. Even so, the religious soul sees more reasons for gratitude in the world than for despair, especially if it can widen its horizon through intercession. Pleasure and excitement are palliatives; thanksgiving is the sole means of really overcoming depression. The author admits, however, that we are often reluctant to take this path to our salvation. "It is strange to reflect that gratitude is such a difficult thing, and that thanksgiving needs so much cultivation."[8]

The practical and even pragmatic nature of this work indicates that we should not expect it to yield a theory in the strict sense. In

----

[7] Ibid., p. 2.—In classical Latin, *intercessio* denotes the action by which an official could protest against some measure taken unilaterally by one of his colleagues or in certain public meetings. A consul, for example, could exercise a right of veto against another consul with whom he was associated. This right was meant to be a guarantee that decisions taken would be collegial in character. In our time, although the word has lost its ancient meaning, religious intercession still denotes a convergence and a conjoined action of several wills. It differs inasmuch as it is less concerned with correcting or opposing others by means of ourselves than with saving them and ourselves through God.

[8] Op. cit., p. 6.

Friedrich Heiler's book, *Prayer*, however, we are given a genuine typology. He first studies what he calls primitive prayer and then proceeds to contrast two kinds of prayer—mystical and prophetic prayer. "The difference between mystical and prophetic prayer", he explains, "is manifest in every way: in motive, form, and content, in the conception of God and in the relation to God implied and in the standard of prayer."[9] Mystical prayer aims, often by means of brief ejaculations, at attaining a wordless contemplation or an absorbing ecstasy; prophetic prayer springs forth spontaneously and violently, it does not aim at the silence of untroubled calm or at the experiences of rapture in the supreme good; it is wordless only by accident as the result of an overwhelming emotion. "In the former, there is silence undisturbed by emotion, or a mind steeped in contemplation, in the latter, an 'outpouring of the soul', a 'crying unto God out of the depths'."[10] The God of the former is either the supreme One, or else a personal absolute, sometimes an impersonal infinite, but always, ultimately, a static Good, whereas the God of prophetic prayer is living, an avenger, anthropomorphic. The former is above history, the latter is active in history. Mystical religion is more feminine, prophetic religion more virile; the one leads us to union in love or even to quietism (and, in extreme cases, to nirvana), the other summons us to take part in the struggle for God's interests among men and for the transformation of the world. "Certainly the innumerable contrasts between these two types have been lessened and bridged over in history, most splendidly in Augustine and Francis, but they cannot be wholly ignored. 'Personality-affirming' and 'personality-denying' religion, the experience of God which values history and that which ignores it, revelation and ecstasy, prophetism and monasticism, transformation of the world and flight from the world, preaching of the Gospel and contemplation— these contradictions are too great to give us the right to assert an essential identity of both types."[11]

[9] Friedrich Heiler, *Prayer*. A Study in the History and Psychology of Religion, London, 1932, reissued 1958, p. 283. He develops here an idea that was implicit in Kant and Harnack.
[10] Ibid., pp. 239–40.
[11] Ibid., pp. 170–1.—It would be an exaggeration to say that in Heiler's view

Lastly, the rules governing these two forms of spirituality show the same contrasts. According to a procedure which Heiler says is discernible in all the great religions, prayer leading to ecstasy has its preparatory stage in meditation, and passes through the ascetic and illuminative ways before arriving at the unitive way. The rule of prophetic prayer, on the other hand, is to escape from rule altogether; it is a simultaneous manifestation of the freedom enjoyed both by divine grace and by men. This prophetic prayer really forms the original contribution made by Judaeo-Christian spirituality; it abandons the refinements elaborated by the various kinds of philosophical spirituality and rediscovers the course of primitive prayer which it intrinsically renews. It is fundamentally irrational, but also fundamentally self-giving.

André Néher has also attempted to arrive at a definition of a prophetic type of prayer. He is far more precise and moderate than Heiler. According to him this kind of prayer in fact arises when a prophet is not prophesying, i.e. when God ceases to make his presence and his message felt, and is silent or is himself now questioned. The prayer of the prophets is a human word that exists *alongside* a word of God. It thus presupposes that man does indeed stand before God, but feels himself to be set back at a distance from the divine mystery; he is, as it were, troubled and annoyed by the divine silence that indicates something he cannot explain. When Job

----

one of these types represents the Catholic tendency and the other that of the Reformation. He does hold, however, that denominational emphasis is evident in these two forms of spirituality. His attachment to the prophetic type seems a partial explanation of Heiler's own resistance to the claims of the Catholic Church to which in many respects he is strongly drawn.

Similar ideas lie behind the well-known study by the Lutheran bishop A. Nygrén, *Eros and Agape. A Study of the Christian Idea of Love*, London, 1932 (and later reprints), and the works of Denis de Rougemont, *L'Amour et l'occident*, Paris, 1939, or *Politique de la personne*, Paris, 1946. In my view, however, these ideas had previously been suggested—in a less polemical form—in a book now forgotten, that contains many admirable pages: A. Sabatier, *Esquisse d'une philosophie de la religion*, Paris, 1898. Consider, for example, the following passage: "Prayer ascends from our condition of affliction and oppression and in doing so, delivers us from it. Religion is quite as much an act of freedom as a feeling of dependence. The sense of my crushing defeat becomes a joyful awareness of victory. The power that humbles me is also that which lifts me up, for it enters into and energises my soul" (pp. 25–6).

is faced by the inexplicable, he prays. When God appears, Job stops praying; he is silent, and covers his mouth with his hand. Thus to pray means to put a question to the Lord. But God *needs* to have man put this question. In the robust and naïve language of the Old Testament, the dialogue is necessary for God's enlightenment. "The prayer of Jeremiah was not the result of the divine presence, but of its absence. And it was this prayer that brought God back."[12] But in order to have a rather better understanding of the mystery of God, the prayer of the prophet must be integrated into a more inclusive setting—that of the prayer of Israel as a whole.

The contrast between mystical and prophetic prayer as drawn by Néher is much less clear-cut than that which Heiler makes; we should note, however, the function attributed by Néher to the idea of distance and questioning and the opposition between silence and dialogue. Our criticism of Néher's book is far less radical than that which we have to make with regard to Heiler's excessively comprehensive, cut-and-dried theory. Both authors agree in emphasising correctly the personalistic character of prayer and also the dialectic which all prayer addressed to a living God must entail. Since it is a dialogue, comprising petition and response, prayer is a dramatic issue, a movement whose elements are interlocked. Unfortunately, however, Heiler's dialectic is all-embracing. By indulging in a rather rash speculative adventure he has drawn contrasts that differ widely in their nature and not all of which are justified either from an *a priori* point of view or from the facts themselves; the linked ideas that he enumerates are: silence and dialogue, contemplation and action, love and self-assertion, presence and absence, daylight and night, human passivity and divine activity, methodical spirituality and freedom, etc. It is possible to believe that all these dualities are synonymous? Heiler seems to take a delight in spreading his induction as widely as he possibly can, for he is soon discussing attitudes to sin, and the individual or collective nature of prayer; he ends up with a theory of mystical monism and of prophetic dualism. However interesting some of his reflexions may be (for example, when he discusses the eschatological kingdom whose coming is to

[12] A. Néher, *L'Essence du prophétisme*, Paris, 1955, pp. 343–6.

be furthered), it is impossible not to feel that they are a little slick, and Heiler has to keep on pointing out that reality does not provide us with his types in their pure state, but always in some mixed form. Would it not be more reasonable to conclude that genuine prayer always involves both movements? For example, with regard to the kingdom of God, prayer certainly consists in trying to find out in God the way to promote it on earth (the eschatological and prophetic aspect), but it also consists in placing the future in the hands of God (the aspect of mystical self-abandonment). On the other hand, it is not obvious why prayer should not always involve, alternately, presence and absence, or why, to the extent to which it is aspiration after God's presence, and even that presence, the ensuing union should not leave some place for intercourse, a conversation between the soul and God. The forms of prayer spread out from vocal and stereotyped prayer to prayer that is silent and free. But silence also has its dialectic, and true prayer is not an escape, it sustains us in our earthly combat. Miss C. J. de Vogel has recently reminded us how inaccurate is the usual way in which the θεωρία of the Greek philosophers is described as alien to the values of action.[13] In a similar way we might criticise the criticism that Heiler has attempted against what he calls the mystical type of piety.

Certainly the different ends of prayer beget different forms, but these all possess their logic, one that is internal to prayer; for prayer is purified and renewed by God's love for us and our love for him, and this leads to an organisation and a dialectical development whose structure is determined by the activity of God's presence. If some special word had to be selected to designate the originating principle of this whole movement, there is no reason why "mysticism" should not be chosen, rather than prophetism. Everyone who prays feels both very near and very far from God, most eager to be united to him and to work for him. What love provokes is precisely this tension, and it is this tension which is so productive. Heiler

[13] C. J. de Vogel, "What Philosophy Meant to the Greeks", in the *International Philosophical Quarterly*, vol. 1 (1961), No. 1, pp. 33-57. J. Burnet had earlier recalled that Plato "insisted on philosophers taking their turn to descend once more into the cave to help their former fellow-prisoners". *Early Greek Philosophy*, London, 4th edition 1945, Chap. II, No. 35, p. 83.

seems sometimes to be on the point of realising this when he admits that *de facto* prayer includes both of the species he has distinguished and is not exclusively localised in either of them.

There can be no doubt that the Neoplatonic ἕνωσις did prove favourable to a pantheistic conception of prayer, but this seems to have been contrary to Plotinus' own intention, for he does not normally prescribe the absorption of the human person in the One. In any case, St Augustine constantly upheld belief in the living God and the abiding nature of the self in the mystical life. The problem is not that of choosing between unity and duality, but of finding unity in duality. It is in this sense that we must surely understand St Augustine's advice: "Ask nothing of God, save God himself." And it is in the same spirit that we must interpret another passage: "For all of us when we pray are God's beggars, standing at the gate of our master on high. We not only stand there, we kneel down, we beg with tears, hoping we may receive something from him; and this something is God himself." These remarks also indicate the permanence of the prayer of petition, but it is a petition which leads to a participation in the very source of all disinterested love.[14]

[14] St Augustine, *Sermo* 83, PL, 38, 515; *Sermo* 331, PL, 39, 1461. The same idea is echoed by P. Burgelin when he says that beggarliness may have its patent of nobility. "It is not certain that the real beggar is not praying, nor that the pride of the 'Vicaire savoyard' is, in its purity, among the highest forms of spirituality." *Encyclopédie française*, vol. 19: "Philosophie, Religion", 19. 36. 8.

CHAPTER 4

The Justification of Prayer

1. *The Stock Difficulties*

Prayer has always had its detractors who either decried its use or toned down its importance in the name of critical thought. In his Tenth Satire, Juvenal describes the vanity of all human desire: we ask for wealth, power, long life, etc., but if our wishes are granted we inevitably end up disappointed, and as unhappy as if we had not been heard. He then turns to the prayers we address to the gods:

> Should man, therefore, desire nothing at all? Believe me, it is
> wiser to leave it to the gods to decide what befits us, and what is
> useful for us. We ask for what we find agreeable; they give us
> what we need.

Considered in themselves, these lines condemn the prayer of petition as both a lack of piety and a lack of thought: let us leave matters to Providence; it knows what promotes our welfare, better than we do ourselves. This poet of irony did not believe that men could be brought to a sensible view of things. This being so, it is a waste of time for us to pester heaven to grant us unreasonable favours. It is not God's silence that appals this censor; it is human stupidity, and this is incorrigible.

The objections to prayer are usually of a different kind. The philosopher George Santayana has summarised them in a few pages; his magnificent style throws into high relief the banalities he has made his own. The facts, he says, give no evidence that prayer is effective: the most orthodox and hard-praying army does not necessarily win the most battles. If we then turn to speculative thought, the conclusion is no more favourable to prayer than is experience. God must know our necessities before we ask and, if he is good, he must already have decided what he would do for us. It follows that prayer can only have a conventional and, as it were, theatrical value, but no moral value. If the course of nature is blindly determined, I may still retain certain ideal preferences intact in a world where values count for nothing. If, however, its predetermination is providential, my prayers are not only without any practical result, they are also impertinent and sacrilegious. It is not for me to ask that the kingdom of God may come, but merely to take notice that in fact it has come. Prayer vanishes in face of dogma. But if we suppose that our prayers do have practical results, the outcome is no more satisfactory. For religion would then become a superior form of magic, a mystical industry, a technique for exploiting the world. Santayana rejects such an idea with horror. For in that case piety would only produce results by becoming mechanical, whereas it must surely have a nobler destiny than that. "In rational prayer the soul may be said to accomplish three things important to its welfare: it withdraws within itself and defines its good, it accommodates itself to destiny, and it grows like the ideal which it conceives."[1]

It would seem that both Juvenal and Santayana proscribe petition only; they authorise contemplation. It is strange, however, that they have not envisaged anything between these two. Santayana, in particular, eliminates every form of invocation, without a word of warning or explanation, and accepts only the soliloquy of the sage. Because merely utilitarian prayer is to be reprobated, he forthwith jumps to the conclusion that each soul is a solitary in the world. Another surprising characteristic of these objections is that their negative conclusions are only applied to religion and they fail to realise that these will also have disastrous consequences in the natural order. If human desires are futile, as Juvenal affirms; if the claim to alter the course of things is absurd, as Santayana suggests; then, we may ask, must not the rejection of prayer be followed by the extinction of all human activity? The only thing left to do would be to speak no more and act no more, if such a renunciation were a logical possibility. In short, we are confronted by a form of *argumentum pigrum*. The *a priori* rejection of the prayer of petition is

[1] I. Edman, *The Philosophy of Santayana*, New York, 1936, pp. 157–61; 1953 edition, pp. 155–60.

based upon an argument which would make any use of the machinery of nature impossible; everything is determined, everything is due to fate. As for the assertion that the efficacy of prayer is contradicted by the facts of experience, it is more than hasty: it is not because the most devout army does not always win in battle that we can take it for granted that the infinitely complex question of the practical results of prayer may be dismissed offhand. Santayana admits that prayer transforms the soul; but can the internal and the external, the psychic and the physical be thus sharply divorced? From this point of view alone, the argument *a posteriori* which he proposes, remains debatable.

Ancient and modern difficulties can in fact be reduced to these two stock objections: (1) To pray means that we accept a childish idea of the real course of things; the determinism of events cannot be altered; (2) To pray means that we have formed a too human idea of God; it presupposes that he does not know our needs before we lay them before him and that his will can be influenced like that of a capricious king.

Theological studies have concentrated mainly on countering the second objection, and rightly; for the fatalistic view of providence which it implies, in a sense includes and adds emphasis to the deterministic view of nature of the first objection. St Augustine, in his *Letter to Proba*, makes this profound reply: God does not ask us to tell him our needs in order that he may learn about them, but in order that we may be made capable of receiving his gifts. St Thomas Aquinas, in his *Summa Theologica*, follows Origen, and maintains that prayer in no way involves a denial of the divine changelessness, for God's mind does not change and is not affected by any outside influence. We do not pray with the idea that we are going to alter what God has decided to perform; we pray in order that we may obtain what he has decided shall come about precisely through our prayers.[2] But the *Dictionnaire de Théologie catholique*, which quotes these well-known passages, agrees that the mystery remains. It seems that some prayers are heard because of their quality, and in such cases, therefore, prayer appears to be a moral cause. It may be

[2] *Dictionnaire de Théologie catholique*, art. "Prière", col. 202–3.

that we tend to over-emphasise in St Thomas's teaching the element of divine foreknowledge and make God subject, as we are, to time past, present and future. As a result the answer to the objections becomes involved in inextricable difficulties. In such confusion Santayana would enjoy a field-day and could repeat his contemptuous remark that the prayer of petition is "perfunctory and histrionic", for God already knows every possible eventuality and the outcome is settled beforehand. And yet it may well be that this view neglects the most valuable elements in the traditional teaching as it was explained by St Augustine and St Thomas. To realise that this is indeed the fact, we only have to consider the problem more directly in that relationship of mutual love which we have seen to be an indispensable element in any philosophy of prayer.

2. *Prayer and Personal Development*

We must unhesitatingly begin with the idea that prayer, whether between human beings or between man and God, is the law that governs personal relationships and that it is by virtue of that law that the praying mind develops. Self-development demands that we should petition others, and this petitioning is the cause of self-development.

(1) It follows that if God wants us to pray to him, this is in order that we may become aware of him and of ourselves, i.e. that we may achieve our own real being, and this implies an openness to all reality. God's grace which summons us to pray, works in unison with the free activity of our being, with our apprenticeship to autonomous existence. Such awareness is not a luxury, it is essential to personal development. Apart from it man remains a mere *thing*, and might be caught up into the moving belt of unconscious causes. But when we assert that he is bound to pray to God, we are really saying that he is bound to acquire personally and to bring into being the very gift which he has to receive. This is a paradox, but light is thrown on it if we reflect on our experience of the way in which minds communicate, and especially on the awakening of a child's mind as the result of the loving efforts of its parents and teachers. The coming to be of a mind is wholly different from the generation

of minerals, vegetables or animals. One of its laws is invocation, and human beings are "called to the vocative", to this activity of invocation, because their destiny is to become free, and without such invocation they cannot be themselves. In the relation between educators and educated a "parent" mind moves a "filial" mind to the activity of asking or petition, and it protects that activity. *A fortiori* this must be true of the relationship between God and man, for God is not merely a master who modifies a man's being, or brings an element of control into it; he is its creator.

(2) When such consciousness awakes it is not just an abstract or ideal reality. When it awakes it becomes a real cause. Pascal wrote: "God has established prayer to inform His creatures how important is the law of cause and effect."[3] This idea is really a thesis of St Thomas's that Pascal had noted down in the course of his reading. It is a magnificent idea. In the first place it shows how it comes about that spiritual activity has a subjectively practical result: serenity, the increased strength acquired by a believer as the result of his self-recollection in God. Secondly, following on this, prayer has, at least indirectly, a practical result in the material world, and we can see that this increase in power may well form part of a wider purpose, that of making matter malleable to mind and ensuring that the causality of material things takes effect through man. Thirdly, whatever favours may be obtained from God through prayer, they are not extorted from him in opposition to his will. On the contrary, the truth is that we have been raised to the dignity of cooperating with him: we do not alter what he intended, rather, we carry it out inasmuch as our autonomy is his will and because he has, through his grace and our acceptance of it, in a sense entrusted his interests to us.

(3) The uncertain gropings of prayer, the fact that some prayers are not heard or do not deserve to be heard, and that, nevertheless, there is nothing wrong in principle in presenting God with definite and even material requests—all this makes sense if prayer is an apprenticeship and if it is meant to become a reasonable service.

[3] B. Pascal, *The Pensées*. [Trans. J. M. Cohen, Penguin Classics, 1961, No. 659, p. 236.]

This is no atmosphere of magic, but one of a drama whose outcome is the development and liberation of the human soul. When a believer makes a prayer of petition, he realises, in his heart, that it is, more than anything else, a request that he may come to know and obtain what he *ought* to ask for. Greeks and Christians are in full agreement on this point. In the *Second Alcibiades*, Socrates exclaims: "Zeus, grant us what is good, whether or no it is what we have prayed for, and turn away from us what is evil, even though we may have prayed for it." This is also the constant theme of the Church's prayers: "Grant to thy people that they may love what thou dost command and desire what thou dost promise, that so, among the sundry and manifold changes of the world, our hearts may surely there be fixed, where true joys are to be found." "O God, who hast prepared for them that love thee such good things as pass man's understanding, pour into our hearts such love of thee, that we, loving thee above all things, may obtain thy promises which exceed all that we can desire."[4]

Throughout even the most bungled course of a petition, this is the pattern that is formed, this is what counts. That is why a believer whose prayers are not heard, usually continues to pray and seems to be unaffected by the experience of setbacks. It is through the practice of prayer that he comes to know what may fittingly be asked for (supposing it be for a miracle: he will no longer ask for it at the wrong time, but when there is really call for it, as though guided by a divine inspiration).

Praying, therefore, implies that I put myself in the position of one who is willing to learn, of one who does not know, of one who cannot do, everything before he even begins. I will not be childishly proud and mark out *a priori* a limited range of objects for which I shall ask; it is much sounder to ask for anything for which we may spontaneously be moved to ask, provided we do so in a spirit of obedience

[4] The collects for the Fourth Sunday after Easter and the Fifth Sunday after Pentecost. There is obviously a vast difference between such prayers and that which Rabbi Onias is said to have practised: as a petition for rain he fasted and drew a circle on the ground and stayed within it until rain came. There is, however, a certain greatness about aggressive confidence of this kind.

and love. Kierkegaard held that the essence of prayer lies in precisely asking for the impossible. However this may be, we may at
least say that, when we pray, our whole being should go into the
prayer without imagining that we can here and now distinguish
between what is possible and what is impossible. If we possessed so
comprehensive a vision, we should be God himself.

At the same time, it is necessary to remind ourselves, that in the
play of our various faculties, mind has its place. And when reflexion
suggests that some contradiction is present, it deserves attention.
During the war both sides prayed for victory. It would have been
opportune to listen to St Augustine, who describes a believer praying: "Lord, do away with the wicked man", and receiving from the
Lord the answer: "Which of them?"

(4) Prayer assists in the establishment of the realm of interpersonal relations, and it does this especially when it is intercession for
others. It is startling and upsetting to note that Santayana has not
even perceived this intersubjective value of prayer, and that after
having dismissed petition with a stroke of the pen, he at once concludes that any idea of a dialogue with God is inane. It does not
seem to have crossed his mind that there might be anything between
petition for material things which he criticises, and solitary recollection which he praises. But it is no less startling to find that he also
passes over in silence the connexion between the love of God and
man and the mutual relationships of men among themselves. When
we ask God for a man's welfare, we put before God (and ourselves)
what is best in that man; or at least we have come to realise the
element in him which offers a hope for his restoration; we go right
back and see him as a child of God issuing from his Creator's hands
unblemished. This is a very striking reality in the case of intercessory prayer; it is even more so, when it is intercession for our
enemies. When I pray for my enemy, I am praying for reconciliation;
and when I pray that enemies may be reconciled, I have already,
through God's action, reconciled them in myself. There is something
in them that has achieved harmony, and this something only exists
in me and through me. Nowhere else as yet has their ultimate condition been reached. It is a victory, which prayer has already won,

over the divisions of space and time, over human wills at cross-purposes. Prayer is thus the springtime of the world, the flowering of that action which will issue in constructive labour, the seed of renewed institutions. It is poetry, but poetry that as an instrument of sacred power commits us in the whole of our being.

It also leads us to the realisation that no order of things can be final that is not cosmic in extent. It spurs us on to a total view of reality. Even if the suppliant is not aware of it, and gives his petition a much too limited character, he cannot speak to God without widening his human horizon. The spiritual life works as a social force. It may suffer counterfeits, it may encourage laziness or hypocrisy; but these abuses are extrinsic and alien to its intrinsic direction. It is not the spiritual life that begets egoism, it is the insincere intention to confine the spiritual adventure to empty words. The diseases of the spiritual life may be called exogenous: they spring from the deadly sins that from outside infect that life, and not in any way from the life itself.

Prayer even enables us to enter a zone of human mutuality in which God alone becomes the ultimate bond between men because he reveals to each man the deepest elements of that man's being. Prayer takes place in a region beyond mere surface relationships; the I and Thou it reconciles are not isolated social atoms but beings in need of indefinite and continuous perfection. Every individual nature that has not experienced God in prayer remains cut off from itself; every human love that omits prayer loses what is finest and most distinctive in the presence of the beloved. All reconciliation that is brought about without prayer remains extrinsic to those reconciled.

In this way, prayer not only widens the individual's horizon, it lays hold of his inmost being as well. Far from vanishing into the universal he gains a vision of his real self. We often hear it said that the privilege of intellect is that from the particular it can rise to the general. This is a most equivocal idea. General ideas certainly exist; but knowledge, or at least the life of the mind, is not confined to them; no, the mind's real calling is to reach the concrete universal, i.e. the individual made fully intelligible. Even in the physical world an atom is important, in some respects as important as a sun; the knowledge of details becomes coherent through a realisation of the way they are connected; and the worth of beings is not relative to their size, but to the part they play and to what they mean. *A fortiori*, prayer will fashion unity between extremes; for it is concerned with persons, so widely differing from one another, and with what is connected with them.

Looked at from this point of view, what objection can be raised against it? Its aim is a universal human society and it takes the first active steps towards its formation. That society is no mere approximation, as in the secular strivings of social, political or juridical life; it lays hold of the most promising elements in each individual and directs him towards mankind as a concretely existing whole, without separating him from his ontological origin and end. Prayer's kingdom comes at exactly that moment when man is given the responsibility for bringing the creation from which he has arisen, to its fulfilment, i.e. for constituting the cosmos of interrelated minds in the midst of a world of nature that has at last been mastered.

(5) Is it necessary to add that in such conditions the difficulties arising from determinism are no more compelling than those founded on a supposed fatalism? In the last fifty years scientific determinism has taken on a new look; and it is particularly important to note that the new situation of this determinism within a philosophy of mind means that it has ceased to be a threat. The forces involved in our experience are not only physical but mental, and the mind that expresses itself or finds its place in an operational and objective field, does not exhaust its potentialities in this; before discussing the laws that control the mind's activity it should be noted that mind is its own primordial law. Prayer which binds minds together is inseparable from them and is identical with their life. There are no more reasons for refraining from prayer to God than for refraining from intercourse with men; or rather, there are fewer. If there is an example where invocation is the obvious activity, it is precisely that of our relationship with God: for to every being he is less of a

stranger than anyone else and he alone controls its destiny whereas others cannot.

(6) Taking a final glance at Santayana we may note that a critical attitude is indeed essential for the development of prayer, although this does not result in the elimination of a mutual relationship transcending the persons concerned—as Santayana claims it does. It is not only a philosophical critique that demands intellectual control and purification for prayer; the devout life and the spiritual experience from which it springs also require it. The Bible provides an illustration of this, for it is erroneous to imagine that Scripture sanctions prayer of every kind. The Old Testament, for instance, forbids magical incantation. In the book of Habacuc we find this passage (3. 17–18):

> Although the fig ever shall not blossom,
> And although the vines may bear no fruit;
> Although the olives give no yield,
> And the fields provide no more food;
> Although the sheep vanish from the sheepfold
> And no cattle in the stalls,
> Nevertheless I will still rejoice in Yahweh,
> And have great joy in the God of my salvation.

The New Testament is severer still. It constantly commands us to pray that we may receive the mind of God, and in the intention of that mind the kingdom comes first, and all the rest (including miracles) is only added as an extra.

In St Matthew, Jesus says (6. 7): "When you pray, use not vain repetitions, as the heathen do, thinking that their many words will ensure them hearing. Do not copy them, for God your Father knows your wants before you ask him." Here we see the element of truth in Juvenal's criticism, although the gospel does not go on to draw the conclusion that therefore we should not pray. In fact, it takes the opposite view! In another chapter, Christ says outright (20. 22): "You do not know what you are asking." It is true that on this occasion he was personally dissociating himself from the naïve ambition of a mother for her sons; but it is permissible to generalise the rebuke, since he was constantly urging his disciples to pray in spirit and in truth and not to go on mistaking the spirit to which they belonged.

It clearly follows from this that if God always granted us what we ask for, he would sometimes be cheating us of what was deepest in our desire.

The whole of this discussion has tended to show that we cannot attain to communion with God and other men without submitting to an apprenticeship. There is a connexion between the necessity to pray and the uncertain gropings of the actual prayer: these two things are not mutually exclusive, as some people imagine, either because they are in too much of a hurry to get to paradise, or, for the contrary reason, that they want to stay on earth and banish God from it.

The history of religions provides us with evidence of prayers of the most varied value. Every society, every century has its own. We are born within a social group and we learn to repeat its prayers. They take different forms, and represent different stages of development. The spirit of religion requires that we should sift and interpret them, gaining inspiration from some, correcting others. A liturgy represents an inductive critical effort of this kind which issues in the establishment of a stable social prayer and yet also to some extent remains open to deliberate renewal. This is because the first movement in which we liberate prayer from its empirical substratum, from its adulteration by magic or superstition, is linked with another in which prayer begets new forms in conformity with the requirements of its inner essence. The apprenticeship is thus twofold. And this is nothing but a general condition of personal life: we emerge from one environment and we create another; we both "receive from" and "act on". But what we receive from outside we have to judge by a higher standard. It is the dignity of the human person that in him all trends and currents meet, and that it is his privilege either to ratify or to reconstruct the very society in which he was born.

Up to now we have examined prayer addressed to God as though it were a matter of connecting the isolated individual with his Creator. We noted indeed that it is a social force, but we shall now see that this is not saying enough and that prayer can issue from a community without losing its inward spirituality. This is the aspect we shall consider in the following chapters on Christian prayer.

CHAPTER 5

The Originality of Christian Prayer

The prayer of a religion that has been in existence for two thousand years is a vast subject. In this chapter all we can do is to make soundings in an ocean. We shall do this by asking three questions: Does the originality of Christian prayer reside in the novelty of its "language of gestures"? Or in some intellectual principle of assimilation and synthesis? Or does it lie in the spirit and object of prayer? We shall thus proceed from the periphery to the centre of the problem.

1. *This Originality hardly lies in the way in which Prayer is Expressed*
The variety of languages used by the human race is immense; almost three thousand have been counted and these are divided into more than twenty-five families. In contrast with this, the uniformity of the "language of gestures" is astonishing. Wherever on earth one may be, it soon becomes easy to grasp the meaning of a sign, provided the thing signified is sufficiently simple. Even when the ideas are subtle and the ideology elusive, a gesture can often bring understanding. Even so, gesture is not always miming. Looking at the matter as a whole, it would seem that in the make-up of all men there are a number of natural symbols, whether reinforced by custom or not, that are always on hand to transmit messages and elucidate states of mind.

These remarks have a special validity in the sphere of religion, and we must expect to find the same elements of physical expression widely present in all religions. A German Benedictine, Thomas Ohm, has made a minute study of the question and its result is conclusive: the originality of Christian prayer is, on the whole, not to be found in the adoption of previously unknown gestures; it can be unravelled only indirectly through analysing the content of its religious attitude.

If one travels from country to country and from one people to another [he says], the number of religions and the contrast between them is remarkable, but what is also remarkable is the widespread unity in the use of the same religious gestures. A very great number of these gestures, and among them the most important, are common to practically all peoples and all religions. Even religions that are profoundly different from each other, such as Buddhism and Christianity, have many gestures in common, e.g. the hands joined in prayer, and the blessing given with the right hand. Taken all in all, in spite of their conceptual and linguistic differences, the religions of the world have their own specific gestures only to a very limited extent.[1]

Christianity retained, in a number of instances, an alphabet or morphology of gestures which was familiar to the religions of the peoples among whom it originated, e.g. the bowing of the head or shoulders, hands extended to heaven, eyes cast down in recollection, etc. Each of these attitudes certainly assumes slightly different forms according to sex, social class, race and ideological grouping. But these are not more than variants.

In other instances, the Christian religion eliminated the gestures that were customary in its early environment. Sacred dances, for example, are a feature of many primitive religions and they were far from unknown in the Graeco-Roman world or even in the Old Testament. And yet throughout the whole history of the Church, they occur only episodically and exceptionally. *A fortiori*, this is true of the acts of breathing (i.e. blowing upon) or spitting. In the mysteries of Sabazios, saliva had an important function; in the gospel narratives it is still evident and we find it disturbing; but in the modern ritual of the Latin Church, it is practically non-existent. For various reasons, the Church has rejected some customs, confirmed others, and held some to be dubious. But elimination has its limits, and there is no prayer unaccompanied by some bodily attitude. Even among Protestants, who insist on a very great simplicity in ritual behaviour, the head is bowed during meditation, eyes are uplifted in invocation, and they stand erect when they say the Creed

[1] T. Ohm, *Die Gebetsgebärden der Völker und das Christentum*, Leiden, 1948, pp. 30–1.

or sing the hymns of their faith. Complete stillness itself implies the adoption of a gesture that is a sign and one that is universally understood.

It has happened, of course, that often enough during the ages, the Church has incorporated a particular ritual act only after considerable delay, because it might have appeared to be a pagan infiltration, or because it seemed to her less suitable than others to express Christian feelings. Thus, for the first thousand years, particularly in the East, the hands do not appear to have been joined when praying.[2] Even kneeling was for long a private custom or else reserved for penitential seasons; in the public worship of the early centuries it was forbidden on Sundays and during Eastertide. *A fortiori*, prostration before men, e.g. before kings or bishops, was only tardily admitted, i.e. when it was considered that circumstances had so changed that the gesture had lost its idolatrous taint. Before this, Christians resolutely refused to perform an act which they held to be impious, and accepted martyrdom rather than bow the knee to a divinised emperor.

In addition, Christianity has gradually lost the use of some gestures, though this by no means necessarily implies that they were considered to be unbecoming, pernicious or ambiguous. The laying-on of hands was very common in the Old Testament, and again in the New; but it has now only a very restricted place in the Catholic liturgy and has disappeared completely from family prayer. A father who blesses his child in God's name, does not place his hands on its head. We find the gesture embarrassing; in contemporary life it seems to be reserved to faith-healers; we feel it to be vaguely magical, even though its use in the liturgy—a very limited use—conveys absolutely no magical suggestion to our minds.[3]

---

[2] And yet in Mesopotamia, the Sumerians, from the fourth millennium B.C. had employed this as their principal gesture when praying to their gods. Cf. A. Parrot, "Gestes de la prière dans la monde mésopotamien", in *Hommage à Wilhelm Vischer*, Montpellier, 1960, pp. 177–80.

[3] This liturgical use is centred on the priesthood. In its new context of Christian ordination, it retains something of the Jewish *samakh*, "the pouring of one's personality into another being" (as in the transmission of Moses' power to Joshua). Cf. D. Daube, *The New Testament and Rabbinic Judaism*, London, 1956, p. 236. But in St Paul's Pastoral Epistles this gesture applied to a man bestowed

If we take into account only the above reflexions, the chief originality of Christian prayer appears to have been that of simplifying the vocabulary of religious gestures. But Christianity has also been creative, not only in the syntheses of gestures contained in its liturgy, but—and much more importantly—in the adopting and fixing of elementary signs. In the first place, it has given a new symbolical meaning to ritual actions which may have been in use elsewhere. Origen, for instance, in his treatise on prayer, asks in what direction we should look when we are speaking to God. "Of the four cardinal points, North, South, East and West, who can fail to see at once that the East shows clearly the direction in which we should pray, for to turn this way is to symbolise the soul's looking towards the true light."[4] To turn towards the sun was a pagan custom, while Jews turned towards the Temple. The New Testament ignores or excludes any specific direction in prayer. But, about A.D. 200 the custom of turning towards the rising sun is firmly established, and the motives given for this are specifically Christian.[5]

The Christian innovation also included the re-direction of certain gestures so as to relate them to events in Christ's life, and particularly to his Passion. For instance the arms extended in prayer became an image of his arms on the cross. This probably began as a merely accidental variant of the common gesture; but later, and as early as the time of Tertullian, it had given rise to a symbolical and mystical interpretation.

Lastly, there is a very important example, in which the symbolical sign arose almost *ex nihilo* in order to express a dogma, as the result of a deliberate and definite intention. This is the sign of the cross.[6]

some function in the Church upon him. Cf. A. Hamman, *La Prière. I: Le Nouveau Testament*, Paris, 1959, pp. 205–7. The laying-on of hands also occurs in confirmation and is related to the priesthood of the laity.

[4] Origen, *De Oratione*, 32, PG, 11, 556–7.

[5] On the history of orientation in collective prayer and in religious architecture, cf. an article by C. Vogel, "Versus ad Orientem. L'Orientation dans les Ordines romani du haut moyen âge", in *Studi medievali*, Anno 1, No. 2, December 1960, Spoleto, pp. 447–69.

[6] It is not however a creation without roots and without a history that suggested it. The prehistory of the sign of the cross may perhaps be seen in the symbolical use of the letter *taw*, the last letter of the Hebrew alphabet (just as *omega* is the last letter of the Greek alphabet). According to Ezechiel, the *taw* is

It was meant as an illustration of belief in the Trinity, and at the same time it reminds us of the redemptive incarnation and of its saving power. This remarkable and very early creation[7] is an instance of a specifically Christian gesture, the direct result of a conviction. The need for expression produced a new and characteristic form that had the power to summarise the spirit of a religion with inspired simplicity and to become the rallying signal for millions of men throughout time and space.

In spite of such innovations as we have mentioned, the list of specifically Christian gestures in prayer is short. The originality of Christian prayer is in fact not to be seen, or only slightly seen, in what we have called the alphabet of gestures. Analogous conclusions could be deduced from an examination of the symbols analysed by Mircea Eliade or of the unconscious archetypes enumerated by Jung. To the extent to which the theories of these authors rest on real and verifiable facts, they imply that we have within us a stock of psychic structures, and notably of ancestral images, with which Christian spirituality cannot fail to be concerned. Nevertheless it is not to be defined by them: if it were, it would be bogged down and perish. A plant needs humus; but the flowers it produces are not humus.

2. *The Originality of Christian Prayer is seen more clearly in its Ends as revealed in its Synthesis*

If we take up our position within that same context of theism that was ours in the previous chapters, we already have a clue to the new factor which Christian prayer has contributed to the phenomenology of religion. From this point of view it is as though Christianity had

the sign of Yahweh that will be marked on the foreheads of the messianic community, and Jewish pietistic circles at the beginning of the Christian era seem to have made use of this *sphragis*. Cf. J. Daniélou, *Primitive Christian Symbols*, London, 1964, p. 140.

[7] The large sign of the cross with which one signs oneself seems to be later than the small sign made on the forehead and the heart or upon external objects. In so early a work as the *Apostolic Tradition* we read: "Take care always to sign your forehead worthily."

From the beginning of the fifth century, we find the crucifix placed first in the apse and later on the altar, as a triumphal cross intended to symbolise and head the triumphant return of Jesus at the parousia. C. Vogel, loc. cit., p. 455.

brought order into the religious soul by disclosing a principle of synthesis and a proportion. Often neither the content nor the method of prayer appears to be radically new; for example, prayer for one's enemies or the contemplation of God's presence in the poor and the sick may well have been taught now and then by a spiritual writer of a non-Christian religion and may not be exclusive to the gospel; but Christian prayer is distinguished less by something absolutely novel than by a controlling theme and by the balance it effects between all the varieties of religious expression.

A number of writers have understood the greatness of the Christian revelation or of Christian prayer like this. C. S. Lewis, in his *Miracles*, accounts for the religious myths of mankind as reflexions of God in the soul constituting a kind of obscure and off-beat revelation. The Old and New Testaments decant and clarify God's image in us. They teach us how to rectify our instinct for God, and to pray in spirit and in truth, but the basic elements were there already. C. S. Lewis, unlike Romano Guardini, does not emphasise the contrast between myth and revelation; in fact he tries to relate them as closely as possible.[8]

Even more suggestive is L. Cognet's essay. He distinguishes four types of personal relationships between the divinity and man: magic, petition, adoration, mystical union. The relation involved in magic must be excluded from Christian prayer; but that prayer shows itself able to harmonise the three others and to allow them to develop together. Therefore, even from the point of view of a phenomenologist or an historian of religions, a strikingly original element in Christian prayer becomes evident from an impartial study of the facts. The author considers that non-Christian religions hardly succeed in developing petition, adoration and mystical union in harmony: any of these forms tends to drive out the others; Christianity alone has succeeded, or at least has alone perfectly succeeded, in ensuring the co-presence of these relationships between God and man. "Putting magic on one side—because it is in

[8] R. Guardini, "Le Mythe et la vérité de la Révélation", in *Recherches de science religieuse*, April–June 1950. Myth is earthly, it expresses the reality of fallen man. Revelation is the answer to myth, it makes use of it only to transcend it.

opposition to its fundamental nature—Christian spirituality assimi-
lates all types and forms of prayer, without being troubled by any
incompatibility, without finding any antinomy between them. This
is its great originality: its power of synthesis by means of which it
gathers together within a single reality elements which, elsewhere,
show themselves to be more or less exclusive of one another."⁹

A partial demonstration of this thesis, or rather of this working
hypothesis, is relatively easy to make when the author analyses
Christianity and the way it has managed throughout history to keep
the three above-mentioned tendencies together within the unity of
its own being. This co-existence also has a logical basis: the up-
holding of the loftiest idea of God is no obstacle to petition; on the
contrary it gives petition a nobler content and a discipline; the up-
holding of the call to mystical union involves no evasion of what
binds us to the Church; on the contrary, it ordains sacramental life
to contemplation, and ensures that contemplation will not turn us
away from the service of mankind in the Church. L. Cognet emphasises the fact that the mystical life is the normal development of
baptismal grace; he quotes theologians of very different schools, from
Fr Garrigou-Lagrange to Henri Bremond, who agree in holding
that all Christian prayer is potentially mystical. And he believes that
the great Christian mystics, even those, like Master Eckhart, who
seem to have become independent, are in reality profoundly influenced by their membership of the Church and cannot be understood
apart from its essential dogmas. R. Otto had previously arrived at
the same conclusion from a comparison between Master Eckhart
and Sankara.

It would seem, therefore, that Christian prayer is endowed with
a power of practical synthesis the success of which is all the more
remarkable because it owes nothing to chance, but is the result of a
conscious and constant internal drive. But when the author adds
that the other great religions have come to grief precisely where
Christianity has succeeded, he gives his argument an apologetic twist
that would demand a lengthy historical investigation beyond his

⁹ L. Cognet, "Originalité de la prière chrétienne", in *La Prière*. Cahiers de la
Pierre-qui-vire, Paris, 1954, pp. 225–6.

possibilities and which will always be open to dispute, if not indeed to vehement objections. So long as we keep to a quasi-abstract comparison between the ends of prayer as shown in its expression, the originality of the Christian religion can indeed be half glimpsed; but that this can be absolutely demonstrated is by no means certain. For this reason we shall try to make this originality clear by a different approach, by examining what Christianity, by definition, has as peculiarly its own, i.e. belief in a concrete mediator who is Christ.

3. *The Originality of Christian Prayer lies Principally in its Recourse to Christ the Mediator*

As an aid to a better understanding of the special meaning of mediation in Christianity, it will be helpful to see what it meant in Greek religious thought.

In his *Nicomachean Ethics*, Aristotle says that all things contain some element of the divine. An English commentator of the last century, Thomas Taylor, after noting that this remark is in accordance with the spirit of Plato, suggests a theory of universal mediation, which can assist us in our approach to this subject. It seemed to him that the beings of the universe form a kind of chain in which each intermediate link transmits a divine influx to the link following it after itself receiving the influx from the link preceding it, but without its being conscious of anything beyond this restricted horizon. One immense purposive movement runs through the whole series and gives a meaning to every event, but the knowledge which each has of it is limited. A modern comparison may illustrate this, that of the Resistance movement in the last war. Within a given network each agent was in immediate contact with only one other member (although even then only under a pseudonym) and knew nothing of all the others. So, in Taylor's theory, every single being is really related to one primary being, without knowing who he is or what he wants. Taylor, in fact, in this passage, is, more than anything else, commenting on a phrase of Theodorus the Platonist: "All things pray, except the first." This axiom also occurs in Proclus. This is Taylor's comment: "Hence, the roots of trees pursue moisture, and avoid dryness; and leaves sagaciously turn from the shade, and joyfully associate to themselves the light of the sun, in conjunction with his invigorating warmth. Through this wonderful sense and appetite, therefore, all things are converted to the first without knowing the first."[10]

Such a view is very different from that of Pseudo-Dionysius, according to which one privileged intermediary, Christ, is able to communicate the whole plan of salvation to men. Even though he sometimes describes Christ as strangely dependent upon the angels, a large sphere of initiation remains possible; the hierarchy of being is not entirely hidden from external observation, and even the secret of the super-essential Principle may be dimly glimpsed in silence. In contrast with this, the kind of Neoplatonism described in the passage from Thomas Taylor, throws us back completely on to the interconnexions and strivings of this earth. Religious prayer is at such a distance from the inaccessible God that it stagnates in the world; it does give sanctity to daily life, but each divine particle is hermetically sealed within its own immediate tasks. All prayer addressed to God in practice flows back to become prayer addressed to men or the contemplation of the natural world around us. It can be imagined what vital support to "humanism" this kind of philosophy of transcendence can contribute. It might even—for extremes meet—give poetry to Marxism and endow it with the spiritual impulse that it lacks without distracting its attention from the world. What it certainly does is to forsake God, it leaves him in an ineffable isolation, precisely because it multiplies the mediators between him and us. The only kind of liberation from our shattered world that we can ourselves achieve is that of doing our duty in the place assigned to us, along a path that is narrow and enclosed by high banks on each side.

The fact is that there are two ideas of what a mediator is. The mediator of the Neoplatonism which we have been considering is indeed able to intercede for the being that follows him in the hierarchy and to transmit to it the special movement received from the being immediately above him. But each mediator dispenses with the

[10] *The Rhetoric, Poetic, and Nichomachean Ethics of Aristotle*, translated by T. Taylor, London, 1818, vol. 2, p. 281.

need to see God; he cuts off the view of the greater part of the horizon to the precise extent to which he is useful to his neighbours; the paradox of the situation is that he diminishes what he receives and what he gives; as it is distributed the message becomes fragmented.

There is, however, a different conception of what a mediator is. In Christianity, Christ does not dispense with God, he dispenses ⅄ God. He at least is able to be complete transparency for the revelation of the supreme principle: whoever sees him, sees the Father. He gives us entry to all things and consequently transforms those whom he enlightens. His mediation acts in an opposite way to the preceding: he does not fall on us like a ray of sunlight in a dungeon, he introduces us to the Father and unveils creation. He reconciles all things in heaven and earth.

In concrete terms, this amounts to saying that Jesus Christ left behind at least two certainties to those who knew him on earth: the first is that he was without sin; and the second is that to all who questioned him he gave an infallible answer in religious matters. Socrates, Sakyamuni, Mahomet did not produce an impression comparable to this, however great they may have been. Exegetes and historians of the origins of Christianity have disputed about a thousand things; they have never produced anything positive that contradicts the overwhelming experience which had Jesus for its object: he was sinless, he held the secret of souls. The impact made on those who were close to Christ during his time on earth was conditioned by many other things also, but these two elements are historically and spiritually decisive in themselves alone. We can never go beyond him, we can only advance within the reality of his spirit, and, as it were, on this side of him, not above him.

This then is the testimony that emerges from an encounter with Christ. This is also, in embryo, the revelation of the New Testament, when the *Evangelium Christi* becomes united with the *Evangelium de Christo*. For is this not the affirmation that Christ reveals God totally? And does it not then follow that he is radically different from other men, in that he is Man-God? When other men reveal God, they also hide him; as mediators we are, all of us, more or less opaque; we can dispense God only by dispensing with him. Christ, on the other hand, dispenses God without ever dispensing with him: his finite nature is no obstacle to the action of the Infinite, it is capable of manifesting everything in itself, since by way of the crib and the cross it culminates in the resurrection when his manhood carried out in fullness that which had united it to the Word from the beginning.

We can now see the essential originality of Christian prayer and what ensures it a unique place in the history of religions. It would be unthinkable to define it without mentioning Christ. Christian prayer is offered "in the name of the Lord Jesus". In his Gospel, St John reports these words (16. 23–4): "Truly, truly, I say to you, if you ask anything of the Father, he will give it to you in my name. Hitherto you have asked nothing in my name; ask and you will receive, that your joy may be full." A Christian knows that his prayer is enfeebled if it is not transmitted through the Word incarnate and that in him it acquires its full proportions because it is in him that creation is gathered into its final unity. It is in Christ that the purpose of all the relationships between persons is at last completed or capable of being completed: created beings enter into communion with their Creator because they have achieved communion among themselves, and they have achieved communion among themselves because they are now in communion with their Redeemer. Beyond this immense dialogue there is nothing; time past is no more, time has reached its goal.

But what do we mean by the transmission of our prayer through Jesus Christ? To pray in the name of Jesus means that we realise that of ourselves we are incapable of perfect transparency, whereas he is that perfect transparency. Sin and error are not in him; therefore we must pray through him, i.e. receive his spirit, conform ourselves to the sinless and religiously infallible Word which he utters and which he is. We have to raise ourselves deliberately to the level to which he calls us. If we fulfil this condition, our prayer will not be too gross or irrelevant. The transmission *per Dominum nostrum Iesum Christum* liberates men and raises them to a level with God. But man cannot reach this position unless he is intimately united to a Man—and this means also to an event—which is our salvation. Once again the enormous separation between Christianity and the Neoplatonism we examined above, becomes apparent. It is our moral opaqueness that makes us inadequate, not our existence in the body. Our mediator has a body and this risen body is no sort of blemish on his divinity, whereas the mediators described by Thomas Taylor actually block out any view of heaven; the matter in their nature is incompatible with the sheer transparency of the One. Even during the three days of Jesus' death, the Church considers that the hypostatic union did not end and that his dead body is therefore to be adored. This dogmatic statement which, in spite of the opposition of some of the Fathers, has come to be accepted, has considerable implications; I do not think it an exaggeration to say that it represents an important date in the history of human belief. Even when we admit the distinction between the Man-God, the unique mediator, and the countless number of intercessors and "dispensers" who have this character only in the imperfect sense of which created beings are alone capable, we do not entirely explain their imperfections by the same reasons as those we give for the imperfections of Neoplatonism's mediators. For Neoplatonism multiplicity is evil in itself; its intrinsic tendency is to divide, and because of this it is "material". For Christians multiplicity may mean communion, and "matter" is not necessarily an obstacle to this.[11]

A host of important consequences follows. Christian prayer which proceeds to the Father through Christ is in liaison with a movement initiated by the Father and present in the world before we began to pray. In fact our prayer is provoked and carried to its destiny by the Mediator. Its first step, therefore, is thanksgiving. It does not begin with the imitation of Jesus Christ, but in the redeeming impulse received from him. When we try to hoist ourselves to his level, our will to do this is itself a gift of grace; we are forestalled by him, he incorporates us in an already existing drama, and makes us part of

[11] Neoplatonists and Christians do, however, agree in holding that the One has a transcendent presence in all things and is not reducible to the unity of a thing.

it. We become incorporated in the supernatural adventure of the world; we are free to enter it spontaneously or to reject it whole-heartedly; we can save ourselves or allow ourselves to be lost, co-operate in the work of the Redeemer or impede its progress. All the same, we are simply carrying on or obstructing something which does not depend on us but on him, and which willy-nilly is written into the very depths of our being.

It is for this reason that Christian prayer cannot dispense with belief in an event—Jesus' presence on earth; nor with a corollary—an obligation to labour for his kingdom. It is prayer based upon a revelation brought by a person and the figure of this person is constantly before it. The protomartyr Stephen is described in the Acts (7. 59, presumably also 60) as, even at that early date, calling on the Lord Jesus, and the first hymns to Christ are in the New Testament. It is true that Origen opposes this custom when he maintains that "prayer is not to be made to the One who prays", but it would be easy to show that even in his case the disciple based his prayer on that of his master and that he found it difficult to pray with his master without praying to him. When we pray with him we are contemplating him, and entering into union with him, rather than appealing to him as to a capricious potentate or a saviour whose fundamental work is not yet done. Of course there are ways of praying to Christ that are worldly; even as prayer to God himself can be anti-religious. And yet how can we exclude from the object of Christian prayer the One who teaches us to bring all minds and wills into mutual relationships and to integrate this universal mutuality into the divinity itself? Christianity is not based upon a doctrine of mediation, however original that might be, but upon belief in a living mediator, and therefore it cannot consider this mediator as a mere instrument. If Christ's function is to throw open to us the ultimate reality in every being, if he shows us a child of God in every man and every man as an end in himself, this can only be because he himself is an end and not a means which piety can dispense with. If he reveals God so totally as to be God, how is it possible to refrain from praying to him as a God? Prayer only develops in a mode of intercourse in which every personal being is worthy of eternal contemplation; in that self-sufficient universe of expression, which, unlike the pragmatic relationships of ordinary social life, is, in its essence, certainly not meant to be "useful for something else", it would be absurd for Christ not to be at the centre of its prayer, since he is the bond between all beings, and absurd that this centre should not be adored on the grounds that he is not the Father. Belief in Christ's divinity implies prayer to Christ; and prayer to Christ began long before the Church had worked out the christological formulae which she considered to be the most accurate expression of her belief in that divinity.

Prayer *in nomine Iesu* really gains its complete meaning only through belief in the presence of Jesus in the Church. It draws us, we said, into a movement that transcends us. Now, this movement is the movement of a new creation; it incorporates us in a renewed mankind, marked by the Mediator, and by him initiated into his purpose of illumination and sanctification. Thus Christian prayer also has a relationship to the Church and the sacraments as a distinctive characteristic. When St Paul writes to the Church of Corinth: "You are one body in Christ", he is bringing the community of believers into intrinsic fellowship with both the body of Christ and the celebration of the Eucharist. Christ's mediation on earth is the originating principle which thus provokes new forms of prayer that are an expression of belief and constitute the liturgy. When we turn to study the aspects of Christian prayer that are expressed in public worship we shall not be leaving, but continuing, the theme of this present chapter. And from this centre to which we have attained we shall be in a position to re-examine the expressive elements we observed above and see them re-vivified. Those gestures that seemed incapable of manifesting the originality of prayer on their own account have now been penetrated by a spirit which gives to their ordering a significance of its own.

CHAPTER 6

The Liturgical Aspect of Christian Prayer

1. *The Life-giving Principle of Christian Worship*

It seems at first sight that the existence of liturgical prayer conflicts with some of the principles that have emerged in the course of our study. We shall try to enumerate these points of friction and see whether the conflict is radical.

(1) The essence of prayer seemed to lie in the fact that it is free and inward; worship, on the other hand, is often vocal and its prayers are fixed; they have only to be repeated. Against this we may reply that the vocal element must always be subordinate to the interior life and that the fixity of the established prayers is meant to be a springboard for the spirit, not a prison. St Thomas Aquinas, in his usual fashion, does not fail, in this connexion also, to develop the educational aspect. But he none the less emphasises that the goal of external worship is adoration in spirit and in truth. External things are ordained to internal realities, the body is subject to the soul, custom is a support to freedom—such is the real order.

(2) But had it not seemed that prayer even on the level of human mutuality had the power of transferring us into a realm of intercourse where sight and sound satisfy all needs, and where communication through touch is no longer necessary? Ought this not to be true *a fortiori* of prayer to God? And yet the liturgy requires much more than the ministry of the word. St Augustine—and Protestants have often repeated his words—called the sacraments visible words (*visibile verbum*).[1] But leaving the possible ambiguity of the phrase —because faith in the divine Word is involved—on one side, it cannot be denied that even for Protestants, baptism and the Eucharist, are celebrated with the aid of water, bread and wine. These material

[1] Louis Bouyer, *Introduction to Spirituality*, New York, 1963, p. 105.

signs are not only contemplated, and a good deal more is done than merely talk about them. The Catholic liturgy will, *a fortiori*, make use of material objects that can be touched. There can be no Christian worship that does not involve handling. The counterpart, or, if it is preferred, the reply to this objection would be the following: no Christian would assert that prayer is impossible without the sacraments, and no suppliant would assert that contact is incompatible with prayer. We did not maintain that prayer excludes touch, but that it could be fully expressive without it, and this affirmation remains true. The sacraments are indeed sacraments of faith.

(3) Lastly, we have hitherto considered prayer, almost always, as a relationship between two minds only. The liturgy, on the other hand, presupposes a collective suppliant; sometimes it supposes that the object of supplication is collective also, as in the Litany of the Saints. Under such conditions, will not the interpersonal relation inevitably degenerate?

This last difficulty leads us to the heart of the problem and enables us to give a better answer to the first two objections. Let us look at it more closely. The risk of degeneration is twofold. First of all, when the suppliant is collective, prayer is in danger of becoming merely an element of crowd psychology, i.e. of showing the fanaticism of false hero-worship or the imperious demands of hypocritical petition. Mob frenzy, lashing its victims, surrenders them to their idol, or surrenders him to them. Will not God be similarly perverted by his devotees who will treat him either as a tyrant demanding wholesale sacrifice or as a prince charming against whom they will clamour if he does not grant what they ask? Moreover, if prayer is directed towards a collectivity, it becomes rhetoric. When Cicero addressed the conscript Fathers, both his own personality and theirs disappeared; all that was left was a cause that had to be made to triumph with every available trick. It is of course true that even between individuals persuasion is not always honest, but mob oratory is always dishonest. The liturgy that claims to have its eyes upon the heavenly Jerusalem may, in fact, be making that Jerusalem earthbound. It may claim to be in a different key, but, in fact, does it not transform the temple into the market place?

We might attempt to answer these difficulties by stressing the pedagogical value of the liturgy as we did above. Kant himself fell back on that. His book *Religion within the Limits of Reason Alone* does not demand the closing of churches. . . . And yet how very much more remains to be said! What must never be forgotten is that for a Christian, Jesus Christ is alive in his Church. That Church is his body. In it a word from God is transmitted and that word is God in action. It is the seed-bed of a new creation. Christ has indicated to his Church the world he foresees, and the Church is meant to be that world in embryo. In this context—and Christian belief can never depart from it—the Church's prayer is, before all else, Christ's own prayer to his Father. We pray *in nomine Iesu.* One of the great trials of prayer when it is a solitary effort comes from its groping character. But in the corporate prayer of the liturgy we possess the certainty of an answer from God in Jesus Christ. It is based on revelation and in fact it is formed from extracts from Scripture. This is its central point of reference, and it provides us with a guarantee against the various forms of despair, illusion or aberration that befall a merely natural spirituality. Man appeals to God and the liturgy answers this appeal by God's own word and by those deeds of God which it promises or proclaims. The sacraments carry with them a special divine grace which is a mode of Christ's active presence in his Church and also a material and spiritual renewal of our human nature. This is the explanation of the vital current that runs through the liturgy: it originated in the past, but is eschatological in direction. It does not enter the arena of secular problems, it offers no economic or social panaceas, its concern is with the creation of new men capable of producing a renewed social life, or, at least, a society in a condition to be baptised.

The fact that Christ's presence in the Church is something above and beyond the resources of nature, far from uprooting the believer, in fact has as its first effect the making of those roots sound. And this is an additional reason why material reality and physical contact must have their place in worship. Nevertheless the realm we have entered really is above and beyond nature, i.e. "super-natural", and hence, although from an external point of view the Church is immersed in the disorders of man and society, it offers to a mind lit up by faith an abiding possibility of holiness, and this delivers it from the trammels of natural existence. Sometimes its representatives may be despicable; that does not alter the fact that in its deepest reality it is one with Christ, who is not kept in thraldom by any of our limitations. It is this that enables the liturgy to be simultaneously personal and collective; it may, for example (though it does so rarely), address itself to the company of the Saints which forms its most glorious sector.[2] It may (and it does so constantly and pre-eminently) gather all those who pray into the unity of Christ. It is an immense society of communicating persons and its activity can continue far beyond the domain of individual petitioning. The liturgy does not suppress such petitions; indeed its structure leaves room for them, e.g. in the moments of silence it observes, or in certain individual prayers, such as those in the Mass before communion. Collective prayer in union with Christ's prayer is in reality an intrinsic source of spiritual freedom and of self-affirmation.

For a non-Christian, these privileges are bound to seem mere dreams, and indeed all we have written about Christian prayer will leave him cold. For the moment, however, we are not concerned with convincing non-Christians, but with trying to understand Christians. The phenomenological justification of their attitude is that it has a meaning. It is perfectly coherent, so long as it has for its object the encounter with Christ in the sacraments of his Church. Granted this, the whole problem is elucidated, and on grounds that are no

[2] If a Christian gives intercession a foremost place in his own prayers, it is not surprising that he should think of the saints as intercessors and that he should appeal to them. But the cultus of the saints may also be something quite different: the contemplation of some aspect of God's sublimity which the saints transmit and which is made more relevant to us in the lives of those saints to whom we feel drawn. It may, lastly, be an expression of our desire to answer the appeal which their lives make to *us* by carrying on and developing what they did. In these three forms of the cultus of the saints we find the components of all spirituality recurring: petition, contemplation, devotion.

The antithesis of a cultus of this kind can easily be foreseen; it is the obsession displayed by some people with criminals. It is a fascination which is sometimes more robust than the attraction of the good.

In order not to paint too grim a picture, I shall say nothing about the invocation of demons which also has always had its adepts.

mere considerations of purely human agreement, no mere clever compromises.

If Christ is present in his Church, then clearly the Church is his sacrament: consequently its worship can be vocal without ceasing to be mental; its services can assume fixed forms without being perfunctory, for they either contain God's response to man's appeal or dispose man to be attentive to that response: its language is not purely intellectual or even exclusively a matter of sight and sound, for Christ is incarnate and not just partly so; its congregations can be vast without becoming a mob, for it is supernatural and creates a kind of mutual relationship in which the group does not crush the individual. Of course a Christian who prays, thoroughly understands that these privileges only exist at the fine point of the Church, and that at its base it may suffer contamination in a world hostile to its vocation. But what the phenomenologist must keep in mind if he is to make an equitable description is the fact that a Christian will instinctively guide his prayer to the spot where that fine point is opening the way to God. A Christian in prayer is not in the least concerned with the banalities of mundane social life; when he takes part in the Mass he is not unaware of the petty intrigues that may go on in the sacristy or the parish, but he is not thinking about them now.

2. The Dramatic Character of Liturgical Prayer

At the centre of Christian worship, and particularly of Catholic worship, is the Eucharist, because it is the supreme instance of Christ's presence. All the other sacraments, all the canonical hours, all devotional practices, are directed towards that presence, which is "word" in the biblical sense, i.e. not merely verbal language but creative action. With this Eucharist, which it repeats and which enables it to participate in Christ, as the fulcrum, the Church organises the whole of the liturgical year. To the Eucharist it attaches the historical mystery of salvation and, in the first place the Saviour's life.

The dramatic character of the liturgy is due not only to the fact that at the centre of the Eucharist the sacrifice of the cross is present, but also to the further fact that it includes God's whole purpose for the world, as well as all the possible forms of human resistance to or cooperation with that purpose. It is this that makes the liturgy a "mystery" in the sense brought out by contemporary theology. Every believer feels that he has become part of an immense adventure; he is initiated into it through Christ's own prayer; he is taking part in a redemptive operation whose decisive action has been accomplished once for all time, but whose consequences are being worked out with a margin of terribly uncertain possibilities, and in that margin he stands.

In some respects the Catholic Mass resembles a drama. The ministers around the celebrant, the choir, the congregation—all this suggests the theatre of the ancient world. Even in the structure of the holy sacrifice there is first a tragic development and then a consummation. Throughout its whole text the Mass sums up an age-long moral and religious experience of mankind. It also, and principally, commemorates, by the *lectio divina* and the symbolism of the ceremonies, those events which were worked out and accomplished in the person of Jesus. In this way it re-presents the past. But it is also an action and it involves participation; it is substantially different from something watched on the stage or from a morality play. The people in the nave as well as the priest at the altar are present on Calvary. They are not playing a part in a drama of the imagination; they are close to Christ and indeed in Christ. On each occasion they draw from that well of living water which sprang from the life and death of Jesus. Communion, more than all else, presents this hidden reality of the Mass, although participation in the sacred mystery is not confined to any one moment of the liturgical action. The altar does not obliterate the nave and is not divided from Christ: behind the outward image there is the existence, several existences and levels of existence, which suddenly enter into symbiosis.[3]

The Latin liturgy brings out clearly the work of Jesus and enables

---

[3] H. Gouhier, *L'Essence du théâtre*, Paris, 1943, pp. 208–14, analyses a form that is midway between the Mass and the theatre, that of the "paraliturgical mystery". Modern examples of this were composed by Henri Ghéon, for example.

those taking part in it to enter more intimately into the drama of his life. The liturgy of the seasons narrates the history of salvation, and that of the saints is unfolded day after day in the Mass itself. In this way the course of the Church through time comes to be incorporated in the mystery of Jesus. The Byzantine liturgy, in its turn, also exhibits the transformation of man by Christ. For Christ is not only an object of worship, he is the way and also the means of travelling along the way. And yet created beings are related to him through a vertical symbolism in which everything is given, so to say, in an instant. The iconostasis, which shields or screens the holy things from profane attention, does not block the converging prayers; it bestows majesty upon the theophany which follows the order of Christ's life and which is unfolded in the sanctuary while the people sing their litanies. At the start of the ceremony the deacon censes the icons, and salutes the saints as "guests come to the sacramental feast, as in Christ all live and are not separated".[4] In both traditions, worship unites the doctrinal and prophetic aspects of the message; it is "kerygmatic", although the improvisations of the early Christian assemblies are no longer allowed. This kerygma is lived by every member, and every member is given a share of responsibility for the spiritual destiny of the world.

It has been held that tragedy denotes a fatal chain of circumstances or of external forces which bring the hero to disaster, whereas drama implies an intrinsic development and involves only the decision taken by the hero. In literary history a distinction of this kind has frequently been made either to contrast external constraint with the necessity arising from spontaneous choice, or to contrast overruling transcendence with personal freedom, or lastly, to contrast affliction that is merely undergone with sorrow that is deliberately sought. In this respect also the eucharistic liturgy is something quite different from any literary form. First, it is good news as a life experience and it does not allow misfortune to have the last word. Secondly, it harmonises God's determination to save us with human

---

[4] N. Gogol, *Meditations on the Divine Liturgy*, quoted by E. Underhill, *Worship*, London, 1936, p. 272.

freedom to choose; it is both the necessity of love and the liberty of man. Man receives his freedom in it through the redemption achieved by the Man-God.

This explains why the liturgy contains what may be called a variety of rhythms and a graduated series of forms. In its services there are moments of silence and moments of speech; there are actions in which everyone is asked to take part, and special duties entrusted to readers or to the choir; and lastly there is the celebrant who comes towards all present because he is possessed by Christ's priesthood. Then, in its actual structure the liturgical action is heterogeneous: the material forms of gestures and words, the observable common belonging of the physical elements that are used, are joined with conceptual and affective forms that admit of considerable variation and act differently in each participating member. A pattern of intentions gives a general sense of direction to the prayers of individuals but it cannot completely settle their content or their value. Indeed it might prove quite startling if we could read all that is passing through the mind of each member of the congregation who is praying: what variety there really is behind the apparent uniformity of kneeling forms and hymns in unison! And yet this variety, for all its deplorable disadvantages, is not by any means just something to be put up with; ultimately it is more desirable than regrettable; for it is not the function of the liturgy to do away with personal freedom, but to enrich its spiritual working. Worship is certainly a discipline, but it is not an extinguisher. It gathers together in one and the same action, Bossuet and Fénelon, a don and a bricklayer, sinners and the righteous. It gathers them together in order to divorce them from the devil and to effect a renewal of their real personality, that which comes from God.

3. The Twofold Movement of the Liturgy

The liturgy as a whole is characterised by an intermingling of divine and human forms, and this fact enables us to grasp the law of its formation. In the first place, the Church collects and sifts the prayers it finds in use about it at its arrival. Our observations on the "alphabet of gestures" are valid also for the syntheses achieved in worship. In the Latin liturgy, for example, in spite of its complexity and the additions made during the centuries, all that it owes to others is easily recognised. It may be said that its basis is Jewish and its framework Roman. Here, of course, we have no intention of enumerating the list of its debts, and the previous remark is merely a pointer. But specialists have provided us with examples in plenty: "The rule of the three hours of prayer of the daily Synagogue worship was observed by the first Christians (the third hour, Acts 2. 15; the sixth hour, Acts 10. 9; and the ninth hour, Acts 3. 1). In the Synagogue, the *Shemôneh ʿEsreh* (or part of it) was said at each of these three services. In the same way the Lord's Prayer was said thrice daily, according to the *Didache* (8, 3). While it is evident . . . that fixed forms of prayer were used in the early Church, *extempore* prayer also played an important part. It is mentioned in the *Didache* (10) and Tertullian speaks of it in his *Apologeticum*, 30 and 39: *Sine monitore, quia de pectore oramus*. And: *Ut quisquis de proprio ingenio potest*. Herein likewise the Church followed the synagogal pattern. The characteristic marks of the Synagogue prayers are to be found in the prayers of the early Church . . . praise and thanksgiving, especially for the power of God as seen in the Creation, for His guardianship, for deliverance from evil, and for spiritual enlightenment, concluding with confession and prayer for forgiveness." And after mentioning some other features, this author concludes: "The historical reminiscences which occur in many of the Jewish prayers are often taken over by the Church and adapted in a Christian sense."[5]

This basic stratum became more complicated. All we had to do here was to show that the initial movement of Christian piety was to continue and develop Jewish prayer and not to do away with it. But by constantly subjecting all it found to a process of adaptation (and its finds were frequently of much lower value than what it inherited

---

[5] W. O. E. Oesterley, *The Jewish Background of the Christian Liturgy*, Oxford, 1925, pp. 125–6. [We have taken the liberty of correcting Oesterley's reference to and quotation from Tertullian.—*Translator*.] Cf. also L. Bouyer, op. cit., pp. 27ff. Bouyer also notes that the same psalms of thanksgiving occur in all the ancient Christian liturgies in the morning service (Lauds) and in the evening service (Vespers), p. 62. The *berakah* was continued in the Christian Eucharist, p. 31.

from Jewish worship), the Church gave these acquisitions a new form and content, because it used them to express Christ. From the outside it looks like borrowing; regarded more profoundly it is mutation. Consequently, if we examine the transition from the non-Christian to the Christian, we must confess that there is a quite wrong usage being made. A blessed misusage, for if there had not been one, it would be disturbing indeed.

A second movement joins the first. The liturgy creates forms which are its own. Through the development due to monasticism, through the influence of Gaul quite as much as that of Rome, it produced in the West the liturgical masterpieces which we inherit. Gradually in the prayers it built up its beliefs round the original nucleus, so that in the liturgy we can observe the history of two thousand years. The same may be said of the Byzantine liturgy that has followed its own particular path.

So, once again, we observe that the ends aimed at in expression both necessitate selection and stimulate creation. And, in conclusion, we note that it is on its own liturgical past that the Church exercises this twofold function of sifting and renewal. What at first took place spontaneously henceforward becomes a matter of much more conscious reflexion. This does not mean that the reforms of the liturgy in our time are necessarily an improvement on its first beginnings. Spontaneous impulse and disciplined control each has its advantages and its defects. Both of them should, therefore, play their part in this development. Spontaneous impulse originates in faith which is directed to the religious reality in question. Disciplined control springs from the experience of established forms. Instinctive life and intellectual reflexion cannot be dissociated without harm.

The fixed forms of the Church's prayer are thus not so changeless as might be imagined. This is a conclusion, perhaps an unexpected one, which means that the liturgy, like the Church itself, is made for man. The kingdom of God is not simply the affair of an *élite*: it is a call to all mankind, a call all men must answer. Christ who lives in the Church challenges the Church in those men who do not belong to it but who are moved to pray.

CHAPTER 7

On the Heights

To climb up to the heights of Christian prayer is to attempt to describe the mystical life. Nothing is more rash, but I intend to risk it. It is rash for me personally, because I do not belong there. It is also rash because those who seem to belong have given rise to very different descriptions of it and themselves seem to vary considerably in their accounts of it.

By *mystical life* may be meant a personal relationship with God. A mystic, in this sense, is a man who, in some way, may be said to be in a familiar relationship with God's mysteries; his knowledge, consequently, has something secret about it, secret not as arbitrarily concealing a truth that should be common property, but rather in the way in which two close friends know each other; between them a special relationship exists that cannot be exactly expressed outside it. The mystical element would thus be equated with the personal element in religion, and it would be principally manifested in an habitual disposition to pray, or in certain peak moments of prayer, thanks to which a believer concentrates upon his God, or is laid hold of by him in a way that leads to greater intimacy.

Is such knowledge mere conjecture or a conclusion from scattered observations, or is it a real experience of the being of God itself? This is a problem we can set aside for the moment. Provisionally, we can also refrain from enquiring whether the mystic's intimacy with God is due to his own effort or to the influence of God's grace acting either gradually or by *raptus*. We need only remember that a mystic is in fact intimate with God or with the things of God, in a way that is entirely personal and hence irreplaceable. Personal originality is thus seen to be a necessity in religious life and especially in prayer.

It is really to this kind of definition that the following passage by K. E. Kirk refers: "I use the words 'mystic' and 'mysticism' . . .

to denote a type of religious thought which believes personal intercourse with the divine to be possible to man (whether it advocates
sacramental methods or not), as distinct from what Johannes Weiss
(*Das Urchristentum* . . .) calls 'Lord–Slave' or 'I-and-Thou' religion, in which God (Christ) and the believer are strongly differ-
entiated, and the only relationship conceived to exist between them
is that of God commanding and man obeying or disobeying."[1]

If, on the other hand, we recall the account given above of Friedrich Heiler, it is evident that, on his premises, mysticism is bound
to be something quite different, and will consist of a union with God
which would destroy the self or the consciousness of the self in God.
Many writers seem to share this view. Millar Burrows, for example,
after discussing whether the members of the Qumran sect should be
considered as mystics, concludes: "There is no indication, . . . as far
as I can see, of that self-absorption, that loss of personal identity in
the divine Unity, which is characteristic of mysticism in the strictest
sense of the word; nor is there any trace of a spiritual discipline by
which the devotee was raised step by step to such an experience."[2]
The principle underlying a statement of this kind is obvious: the
mystical life involves the dissolution of human personality in the
divine. This is why the writers to whom we refer, and they include
Emil Brunner, normally reject mysticism, holding it to be a danger
for a Christian, and perhaps even incompatible with revelation.
Several of them regard it as an inheritance from Neoplatonism
which, on their view, is a form of pantheism. But this aspect of their
thesis need not be considered here, for it raises a problem in the
historical order which is extremely complex. However inadequate
Neoplatonism may be from a Christian point of view, it is doubtful,
as we had occasion to remark previously, whether Plotinus himself
taught that personal identity disappears in the state of ecstasy.

Of the two views we have just described—intimacy with God and
disappearance in God—it is clear that only the first can be harmon-

---

[1] K. E. Kirk, *The Vision of God*. The Christian Doctrine of the Summum
Bonum, London, 1946, p. 27, note.
[2] Millar Burrows, *More Light on the Dead Sea Scrolls*. New Scrolls and New
Interpretations, London, 1958, p. 382.

ised with Christian belief. Nevertheless, it is a fact that Christian mystics often seem to have been attracted by the second. Ultimately, however, they cannot be fully satisfied by either of them. Is not the difficulty due to the fact that language tends to distort their meaning and that their descriptions of prayer have often given rise to misunderstanding? We have used the term intimacy; we can now be more precise: friendship is what is meant and friendship that springs from God's grace. All the mystics share the conviction that they owe their spiritual being to a special action of God who raises them up to himself. In the love relationship which unites them with God, they are begotten by God and enabled to experience him; they are also enabled, in a sense, to beget God by the grace of God. This causality and this intimacy make it true to say that they are divinised: they are only two through becoming one and only one by remaining two. The paradox of this statement can be clarified, a little, only by means of analogies from the mutual relationship that is established when human beings are in love. It is a relationship that can be expressed in a simple formula only with extreme difficulty. In order to grasp firmly that we are in no sense faced with a form of pantheism, it may be well to ponder again the penetrating lines in which R. Otto analyses this mystical duality. This unification is not "of a logical, but of a mystical nature. The word 'is' in the mystical formula of identification has a significance which it does not contain in logic. It is no copula as in the sentence: S is P; it is no sign of equality in a reversible equation. It is not the 'is' of a normal assertion of identity. However much the emphatic pronouncements of Sankara and Eckhart strive to attain to the latter, they do not succeed in hiding the fact that their logic is indeed the 'wonder' logic of mysticism. One might try to indicate this by forcing the language and making the verb 'be' into a medium of higher unity of intransitive and transitive. For instance one might say instead of: 'I am Brahman', 'I am "existed" by Brahman' or "essenced" by Brahman, or "Brahman exists me"."[3]

[3] Rudolf Otto, *Mysticism East and West*. A Comparative Analysis of the Nature of Mysticism, London, pp. 84–5. A similar observation had been made by Coleridge.

Otto believes that his observation applies not only to Eckhart, but also to Sankara. We are not concerned to decide for the moment whether these applications are valid outside Christianity, but they can throw some light on the problems with which the description of Christian mysticism confronts us. We are going to examine some of these. On the heights of prayer what is it possible for us to see? What is it right for us to love? What is it necessary for us to do?

1. *What is it Possible for us to See?*

It is sometimes said that the desire to *see* God comes from the Greeks and is not Jewish in origin. This is a false simplification. One of the merits of the book by K. E. Kirk from which we quoted above is that it has shown the opposite to be true, or, more exactly, has established that Christianity offered the vision of God to a world aching with the hope to attain it.[4] For Christianity, to see God is the goal of the Christian life, and its supreme good cannot be placed elsewhere. But this doctrine had a long previous preparation not only among the Gentiles, through the zeal of the philosophers for the βίος θεωρητικός or that of the mystery religions fixed on the ἐποπτεία; but also, and less equivocally, through the Hebrew piety of the patriarchs and prophets and later in the religious renewal after the exile. Philo calls his people an ὁρατικὸν γένος. It was a development of much complexity. In the early period of the Old Testament, the vision of God is conceived of as physically possible in this life, but as involving instant death. Only a few favoured mortals like Moses were able to attain to it without harm. At a later period the

Another commentator, B. Welte, gives a different account of the identity proposed by Master Eckhart between the νοῦς and its Creator. He holds that it is identity in action rather than in being. "*Gott und ich, wir sind eins in diesem Gewirke, er wirket und ich werde,*" said the Master. Behind these words lie Aristotle's observations on movement, reproduced by St Thomas: "*Unus motus, secundum substantiam, est actus moventis et moti, sed differt ratione.*" In them also may be found the equally Aristotelian idea that the mind (like the eye) does not see itself but sees all things to the extent to which it gets rid of every adventitious element and all opaqueness (νοῦς ἀμιγής). Mystical renunciation is ultimately, on this view, a self-purification, a self-discovery in God, not a form of annihilation. Cf. B. Welte, "Meister Eckhart als Aristoteliker", in *Philosophisches Jahrbuch*, vol. 69 (1961), fasc. 1, Munich, pp. 64–74.
4 Cf. K. E. Kirk, op. cit., p. 54.

passage in Ezechiel about the prophet's vision of a fiery chariot was the subject of commentary. Some rabbis held that four holy persons had been allowed to enter paradise, but only one of them returned safely; the others died or went mad. In apocalyptic literature, as a general rule, the vision of God was postponed to the Messianic era or else considered to belong exclusively to the next life.

Alongside this development, however, there was another, according to which God is physically invisible; it is through his works that he can be known, it is primarily through faith or a mystical and ecstatic experience. Philo's school obviously followed this line. With the New Testament we find these data inherited but transformed through the position it ascribes to Jesus as the revealer of God; in it, mystical experience becomes communion with Christ in the Spirit.[5] It is still an ideal of vision, but with the material element eliminated; God's essence is to be approached by the fine point of the soul. In the words of St John of the Cross in a famous passage: "God has become, as it were, dumb, and has no more to say, since that which He spake aforetime, in part, to the prophets, He has now spoken altogether in Him, giving us the All, which is His Son. Wherefore he that would now enquire of God, or seek any vision or revelation, would not only be acting foolishly, but would be committing an offence against God, by not setting his eyes altogether upon Christ, and seeking no new thing or aught beside."[6]

Although they have received a fundamental transformation, the words spiritual vision or light are still the fittest to match this particular experience. It is, of course, not a goal that can be reached without much testing. Ever since Evagrius Ponticus (346–99), Christian thought has commonly distinguished three stages in a fervent spiritual life: the purgative way, to free us from the power of the passions; the illuminative way, to vitalise us by the word of God; and thirdly, higher contemplation, which is unalloyed prayer or the gnosis of the Blessed Trinity, in which vision experiences God directly. Later writers, or those of a different school, call this third

[5] Ibid., pp. 11–20 and 110.
[6] *The Complete Works of St John of the Cross*, trans. by E. Allison Peers, London, 1964, vol. 1, p. 163.

stage a unitive way or a spiritual marriage: the soul is stabilised in God's love and flooded through and through with the gifts of the Holy Spirit.[7]

Now from the fact that, in its fundamental reality, God's presence is not perceptible by physical sight, it follows that the transition to a wholly different sphere which a believer has to effect, is bound to provoke a series of very disturbing reflexions which are summed up in the doctrine of *mystical darkness*. This time it is to Pseudo-Dionysius that we must turn in order to discover the first masterly description of a state of soul which recurs again and again during the succeeding centuries in both East and West. Here are some of the essential passages: "To the utmost of thine ability, raise thyself into the unknowing until union is attained with that Being who is above every essence and all knowledge; it is in fact by going forth from thyself and all things in a pure, free, irresistible movement that thou wilt raise thyself to the superessential ray of the divine Darkness, having renounced all things and freed thyself from them." When Moses entered into the cloud of unknowing, "he found himself in the intangible and in the absolutely invisible, since he was wholly possessed by him who is above all things, and no longer belonged to anything else, not to himself, not to any other, and was united in the noblest of unions with the Absolutely-Unknowable, through the stilling of all knowledge, and since in that total unknowing, he knew with a knowledge that passes understanding".[8] There is thus an obscurity of unknowing which arises from the fact that discursive reasoning is transcended; but beyond this subjective divesting of the self, there lies the deepest darkness due to the absolute transcendence of God himself.[9]

The mystical life, therefore, will now involve solitude, a frustrated intuition: its God is inaccessible. Dionysius even says: "totally unknowable (παντελῶς ἄγνωστος)". And yet the way of negation, which, according to this school, consists in saying of God what he is

[7] Cf. L. Bouyer, *Introduction to Spirituality*, pp. 77ff.
[8] Cf. *Denys l'Aréopagite: La Hiérarchie céleste*, edited by R. Roques, Paris, 1958. The passages here quoted are taken from the Introduction, p. xxxiv.
[9] Ibid., p. xxxviii.

not, in order to avoid error as far as possible, thanks to this very use of negation, keeps clear of the agnosticism of non-Christian philosophies. It does so because a Christian mystic believes that God has revealed himself; through Christ a likeness to and a union with God are possible for us. Dionysius makes abundant use of these ideas, and especially of that of ἕνωσις: he promises the followers of the sacred hierarchy wherein the message of holiness is diffused, a divinising knowledge through which they will become in Scripture's words on Wisdom, "perfectly transparent mirrors without blemish".[10] It is, therefore, the grace of God that solves the paradox. God is transcendent, but he is not shut up inside that transcendence as in a jail; he can communicate himself, although no one can invade his territory by force. God submits to no compulsion from any created being, but he can give himself from love. Somewhat inflexibly, in a way that in spite of its subtlety may seem clumsy, Dionysius removes the greatness and mystery of God from human ambitions, but he leaves God with the initiative of communicating himself to man. Man cooperates but only to the extent to which he is passive, passive in the very special meaning of that word made famous by the mystics, and that does not denote inertia, but the giving up of all self-sufficiency and the adherence to the very source of all higher energy. Man knows and acts, but no longer with the activity of his own unassisted nature; he knows and acts personally and for his own advancement because he has become as it were bonded to God who enables him to be with him and in him in such a way that, simultaneously, God both operates all things within us and makes us autonomous. Such is the effect of this creation and this life-giving fellowship.

Does this mean that all difficulties are solved and that mystical prayer can now be easily explained? The matter is not so simple. In the history of Christian prayer the tension between the mysticism of vision and that of the night, remains. Two tendencies continue to be observable, manifested in different schools of spirituality, or even within the same school. It must also be admitted that theologians show some inconsistency between when they are describing mystical experience and when they are acting as directors of conscience. In

[10] Ibid., p. 88.

the first case, they usually say that God condescends to make himself perceptible to the soul; they define mysticism in terms of the intuitive experience of the reality of God as it results from a special grace from him; and they even allow that this grace is generously offered to all who are baptised and is germinally present in the faith of the lowliest Christian. But when they have to give advice to Christians, they change their tone completely: they declare that we can have no awareness of the action of grace in us, they cast us abruptly into unknowing and maintain that holiness on earth is not accompanied by the vision of God nor by any consciousness that God is working in us; immediate and direct experience has suddenly become suspect to them.

In order to illustrate this conflict its theses and antitheses may be contrasted in two parallel columns. We give the main antinomies which can easily be discovered in works of religious philosophy or theology, and spirituality, produced by Catholic writers in the course of the last few centuries:

Theses	*Antitheses*
1. The mystical experience is a perception of God. It is symbolised by light and enlightenment: God is near at hand; there are signs of his presence. Ecstasy is a foretaste of heaven.	1. The mystical experience is dereliction. It is symbolised by the night: God is distant; he is not perceptible on earth. We are in the economy of faith and share in Calvary.
2. Mystical experience provides the only convincing proof of God.	2. Mystical experience proves nothing; it is not a proof but a trial.
3. In mystical experience one knows what is happening. The soul can observe its own action and know itself. The activity of grace can also be perceived.	3. In mystical experience, the soul does not understand its prayer. It cannot and should not attempt to know itself. The action of grace is imperceptible.

A fourth may be added to these three antinomies, but since the adherents of the first three theses may be found as supporters of this fourth antithesis, I have kept it apart from the others:

4. There can be no advance towards God without a spiritual method. There can be no mysticism without previous asceticism.	4. The advance towards God primarily demands self-abandonment to his good pleasure and his inspirations.

It is not sufficient, therefore, to appeal to grace as the solution of the enigma of mystical prayer. For both parties agree that a supernatural raising of the soul takes place and, nevertheless, disagree over the awareness we may have of it. Are we to think that personal preferences have been hardened into systems and that the ultimate explanation of these differences is temperament? Or is there an inescapable alternation between light and darkness and have the theorists deliberately stressed one of these phases and minimised the other? Or is it, as we suggested above, a difference due to the point of view, speculative or practical, which the writer is trying to inculcate at the moment? Or, lastly, is the conflict due to the fact that the ideal of philosophers is a speculative system and that of artists is intuition?

There is some truth in all these explanations. But what really is the answer? A Christian must seek it in Christianity and above all in the Gospel. Now there can be no question that the gospel word will be penumbra and not light and still less darkness. In the gospels God is certainly present, with a presence that is intimate, but that may be veiled or unveiled according to circumstances, and which in all circumstances is given to us transparently in Jesus Christ. No one knows "what the Father is, except the Son, and those to whom it is the Son's good pleasure to reveal him" (Luke 10. 22); for "no man has ever seen God; but now his only-begotten Son, who abides in the bosom of the Father, has himself become our interpreter" (John 1. 18). And again in St John's Gospel, Jesus declares: "Whoever has seen me, has seen the Father" (John 14. 9; cf. 12. 45). And yet this same Christ on whose face shone the splendour of the knowledge of God's glory (2 Cor. 4. 6), entered the shadows in Gethsemane and on the cross. We cannot improve on him; our humanity cannot claim exemption from those afflictions that did not spare his humanity.

So it is to a doctrine of penumbra that a consideration of the New Testament leads us. The economy of *homo viator* is that of half-lights and eschatological tensions, the means of our apprenticeship for the beatific vision. Through an intuition that does not exclude reasoning and through reasoning that is meaningless apart from intuition, we are involved in a dialectic of interior progress which is itself bound up with the development of the relationship between persons, for, in the end, nothing is explained without a dialogue and this is the *sine qua non* of prayer at any level.

With these considerations in mind, what are we to think of the way of negation? The element of truth in it is very limited, but we must admit that it has that element. If personal development is a process that is never completed, if the dialogue with God can never stop, then there is a sense in which it is true to say that the deepest reality of our being is still unknown to us and always ahead of us. In the words of Séguenot, the mystic whom Bremond quotes: "Things take place in you which you do not know and God works things in you which you do not understand, and most often it is when you do not feel them, when you do not know them, that they are at their best. There is a part of our soul which is unknown to us and in no sense in our power: this is the ground and essence of the soul. We are quite conscious of what goes on in our understanding and will, but what goes on in that place is hidden . . . and yet it is there that grace is mainly situated and where it lays up the greatest and holiest gifts it confers on us."[11] The mystery of spiritual growth is the result of this beginning, the creative gift of grace, that cannot be perceived. It is this that moved Bremond to write boldly: "Baptism establishes this new-born infant in a state of pure love; the fine point of this little dumb creature is, in some way, an essential prayer, but one that does not pray." Nevertheless this initial act must work for the perfection of our self-hood, and Bremond adds at once that in the soul of the saints, however "inactive" it may be considered to

[11] H. Bremond, *Histoire littéraire du sentiment religieux en France*. La métaphysique des saints, vol. 1, Paris, 1928, p. 129.

be, freedom is exerting itself. "It is no mere phenomenon of habit, a temporary suspension or sleep of the faculties. When an athlete or a mathematician is asleep nothing remains evident of the agility we admire in the one or of the intellectual prowess of the other. The battery remains charged but for the moment the current has ceased to flow. In the saints, however, the current does flow. God delights in following its imperceptible transmission. Phosphorescent darkness, vigilance in sleep. Mid-day of the fine point, night of the faculties; sleep of the latter, permanent wakefulness of the former."[12]

The negative way has in addition the value of being a warning against the temptation to believe that our minds can encompass God. It is related of Aetius that he claimed to know God as thoroughly as any object that we physically see or touch. This insolent familiarity provoked the reply made by St Gregory Nazianzen in his sermons on the incomprehensibility of the divine nature. This is the context in which one aspect of the negative way deserves study and acceptance. We can never have more than a limited idea of what is possible to God: we are brought up short by the obstacle of his transcendent reality; it is absolutely impossible for us to break into that stronghold, though it is possible for him to open himself to us and for us to receive him.

In spite, however, of these advantages, the doctrine of unknowing is dangerous and can rapidly become opposed to the spirit of Christianity. To deny all possibility for the human mind to have some kind of intuition of the life of grace and some grasp of the divine reality is unnatural and would ultimately involve contradiction. The trenchant negations made by some writers can be justified on pedagogical grounds only. For if a person claims that he is in privileged communication with the Almighty, it is wise to be suspicious and to consider him deluded until the contrary is proved.

---

[12] Ibid., p. 100-1.—The birth of our being in God is something that can be known only at the end when our heart and mind have cast aside the blinkers of ingratitude and the hesitations of their development. On the difficulties concerning an intuition of the beginning, cf. the excellent study by Paule Levert, *L'Idée de commencement*, Paris, 1961. Cf. also, J. Mouroux, *L'Expérience chrétienne*, Paris, 1952, which, without naming Bremond, is a reply to him and provides a profound and balanced answer to all these problems.

In this sphere, crude forms of delusion are commoner than genuine mystical experience and this, when it does occur, is accompanied by a sense of humility and reserve. Exalted sensations are a frequent cause of deception, and in any case they should be subjected to a long period of verification and should never induce the soul to bask in a prematurely won paradise.

This fund of experience has resulted in the cautious watchword: There is no intuition of the supernatural! But prudence should not lead to a lack of discrimination, and higher and lower forms should not be systematically lumped together and judged by the learned as a single whole. A misty dawn must not be mistaken for the mid-day sun, but neither must we conclude that we are struggling in stygian darkness. The essence of prayer is communion, not exile. The act of praying is an affirmation that where there are persons with minds there is an inherent tendency to mutual relationship and to a condition of mutual transparency. To deny this, even on the grounds of safeguarding God's transcendence, would be to give up what constitutes the most venturesome and radically original element in the Christian revelation.

It should not be forgotten that this originality cannot be separated from belief in Christ the revealer of God. That which was intrinsically invisible became visible in the incarnate Word. We cannot repeat what we said on this theme in earlier chapters; but the fact should be noted that discussions on mystical knowing or unknowing have often, for some centuries now, been carried on as though Christianity were not based upon an historical Mediator, and as though as a result we did not have the revelation of a mysterious plurality in God, expressed in the dogma of the Trinity.[13] God is not a reality of sense, but he became so in his incarnate Son. The revelation of God which was made by a person to persons, trans-

---

[13] "For some centuries now," I say, because in Pseudo-Dionysius himself the Trinitarian nature of God is strongly emphasised. The precise reason why God cannot be named is that this would mean expressing the Tri-unity in words, and it cannot be done. The super-essence belongs to the Trinity, not to a unipersonal God. $'A\gamma\alpha\theta\acute{o}\tau\eta s$ is the first divine name and it corresponds to the descent of the anonymous into the polyonymous, and this is a mere second-best. V. Lossky, *Théologie négative et connaissance de Dieu chez Maître Eckhart*, Paris, 1960, p. 62.

figures in him the whole realm of creation and leads us to the discovery of divine "persons". If these points were to be passed over
in silence it would mean that any attempt to describe Christian
prayer would certainly be falsified.

2. *What is it Right for us to Love?*

With this second question we meet two extremes it is difficult to
harmonise. On the one hand, many philosophers and theologians
say that the pursuit of happiness is the mainspring of the moral life
and even of the supernatural economy. On the other, over against
this eudemonism we find certain mystics who maintain a doctrine of
holy indifference or even of overt hostility to the world. This means
in practice that they hold that all search for a happy life is worthless.
The apparent contradiction between these two views arises from a
situation similar to that which we noted previously. The same men
pass from one theory to another on one and the same day according
to whether they are speaking as speculative theologians or as
spiritual directors, and fail, apparently, to observe that their succes-
sive statements do not at first sight harmonise.

Eudemonism has been a classical theory since the Greeks and
there is no need to waste time defining it. Its Christian expression
may be summarised in these words: "Seek happiness, and if you
accept the full meaning of this imperative, you will be led to the
kingdom of God." On the other hand, the mystics who preach
detachment say: "Seek first the kingdom of God, and all the rest
will be added to you." Certainly this sounds more like the gospel,
and yet this initial advantage does not excuse us from looking at the
question more carefully.

We are, in fact, now plunged into a debate: that of the possibility
or not of disinterested love, a dispute which has been stirring up
trouble ever since the Middle Ages, and still does today. Once again
it is the *Histoire littéraire du sentiment religieux* that can best help us.
Bremond sides with disinterested love, which he identifies with
theocentric spirituality. He takes it for granted that genuine piety is
theocentric and not anthropocentric. But it would be false to assume
that in his thought disinterested love has anything in common with

the exaltation of feeling and the romanticism of the heart. The real issue lies, as he sees it, in a contrast between mystical prayer and the following two monsters:

(1) The pursuit of pleasure, even if that pleasure means the enjoyment of God in himself or of oneself in God (this, Bremond condemns as pan-hedonism).

(2) The pursuit of moral progress and inner perfection, understood to mean that the spiritual life depends upon an effort of the will rather than upon divine grace (this Bremond condemns as asceticism).[14]

In opposition to these two tendencies, Bremond develops the idea that disinterested prayer, being concerned with God alone, must consist in self-abandonment, passivity, adherence to the supreme will, abiding in that state to which grace has raised us, rather than in a Pelagian reliance on the quantity of our acts and the success of our plans.[15]

Bremond, unlike some other commentators, considers that the writings of St Francis de Sales are penetrated by a doctrine of disinterested love, as described above. With the instinct of an advocate he at once selects a rather terrifying passage in the letters addressed to St Jane Frances de Chantal in which Francis describes the anguish of a singer who became deaf, but who did not stop singing or playing his lute, not for his own pleasure since he had lost his hearing, but to gratify his prince. Then, the prince, "in order to put the love of his singer to the test, ordered him to sing, and abruptly left him there in the room, and went off hunting". "There is nothing sadder than to serve a master who is unaware of one's service, or, if he is aware of it, shows no appreciation of it; in such an eventuality, love must be profound since it depends on itself alone, can count on no pleasure and can make no claim." That is the state of a soul that is

---

[14] There is a third monster, or perhaps better, a third head of the monster: the substitution of argument on our part for the acceptance of the inspirations which it is God's freedom to bestow on us, as though the worth of prayer depended on the outcome of our complicated plans and on our astuteness (this Bremond condemns as intellectualism). But this monster does not concern us here, since it is only indirectly related to our subject.

[15] H. Bremond, op. cit., pp. 89–91.

inspired by disinterested love. Should God withdraw so that he is beyond the range of feeling, the soul will maintain its loving attitude because of the love it bears God for this love belongs to both, and yet it will not deceive itself; it will value this love because it is directed to God and not because it has originated in the soul or is offered to God as a reward. It is devoted not to the consolation of God, but to the God of consolation.

St Francis adds that God, "entering into the soul in order to enable it to die happily to sin and rise to grace, stirs it to give up . . . all sorts of affections for the things of this world; then he moves it to discard its own self-esteem and self-love, and, lastly, he even deprives it of the life (of its faculties), of affection for the virtues, for the spiritual exercises and for the interior consolations which seemed to be its life; and in this way he brings it to its death, to a separation from everything it possessed and from all that it was".

These words remind us of St John of the Cross. They make the same demand for renunciation not only of possessions, but of the self; the same defence of darkness (for darkness and disinterested love are related); they express the same need for a participation in Christ's dereliction on the cross; in a word, the same condemnation of all spiritual gluttony. Such teaching has a masculine beauty that lifts us far beyond the cloying sweetness of an effeminate humanism, and beyond the conventional philosophy of a happy life. It is understandable that it should have become widely accepted—and perhaps distorted—in the great period of French spirituality, as the extracts supplied by Bremond show. Jansenism had practised it before Fénelon. And Barclos, in particular, plunges us into a tragic form of Christianity in which the fire of charity no longer offers the slightest gleam of hope: the ordinary course of Providence is the apparent abandonment of the world by God. Even the Church can offer us no visible consolation whatever.[16]

There have been fanatics of passivity and dereliction. Their

---

[16] L. Goldmann, *Le Dieu caché*, Paris, 1955, pp. 161–81. The uncle of the Abbé de Barcos held a more balanced view, as shown by J. Orcibal, *Saint-Cyran et le jansénisme*, Paris, 1961. But is his teaching consistent? (Cf. pp. 56, 81–2, 114ff.)

attitudes have shown considerable variation, if we are to judge from another and more recent instance, that of Simone Weil, who, in words of delirium, envied Christ on the cross, and, so to say, going beyond even this stage, desired only to be "de-created". She begs God to take everything from her, she asks to be "devoured by God, transformed into the substance of Christ and given to be eaten by those unfortunates whose bodies and souls lack every kind of food. And may I become paralysed, blind, deaf, imbecile and doddering. . . . Father, since thou art Goodness itself and I am mediocrity incarnate, tear from me this body and soul and make them thine, leaving me, eternally, with nothing but this tearing away, or indeed with nothingness".[17]

It would be very wrong to judge any doctrine from the exaggerations to which it has given rise, and the examples quoted are exaggerations. Barcos yielded to a frenzy for self-emptying and Simone Weil was obsessed by suffering. Such persons are great because they proclaimed so openly their hatred of everything that is merely relative. In order to reach the absolute they refused all truck with the world, and, at least in the case of Simone Weil, took up a way of life that committed them to an early death. Nevertheless, a splendid error remains an error, and even becomes more harmful still.

Does this imply that the tendency of the Spanish and French schools of mysticism which is at the origin of this emphasis, or at any rate is apparently in sympathy with it, cannot be wholeheartedly

---

[17] Quoted by M. M. Davy, *Introduction au message de Simone Weil*, Paris, 1954, pp. 175–6. The philosophical problem involved in the attitude of Simone Weil is that of knowing whether the self is negative or not. For Simone Weil it is negative; it can only assert itself by withdrawing some element from being, and in opposition to others. For a philosopher who holds that persons are essentially related, the self is not negative. It subtracts nothing from being, and is never more truly itself than when it becomes universal.

We have indeed observed (pp. 72, 83–5) that when prayer is addressed to God, a created being is moved to alter his whole outlook and to bridle his egoism. But it is one thing to say that he must cease to consider himself as the ultimate, and to add that such renunciation is difficult, and quite another to define personality as an unjust and inadequate centre of claims and protests, in the manner of Simone Weil and some of the mystics.

accepted? Before we answer this question, it would be wise to examine the writings of the masters and see whether they do not contain teaching that contributes to a more balanced view; their teaching is more complex than is usually assumed. The contradictory statements made by commentators on St Francis de Sales show this clearly. His deaf singer is only one episode in God's governance and in man's condition. He does not present it as the model of the Christian's destiny. "Some people ask for the cross, but I do not; all I ask is that I may be ready to carry such crosses as his Goodness may be pleased to send me." And again: "I should much prefer to carry a tiny cross of straw that was put on my shoulders without my choice, than to go into the woods myself and laboriously cut down a far heavier one which I could scarcely carry."[18] All that St Francis asked of his disciples was that they should incorporate God in whatever they desired, even when they had no consciousness of his presence. They must be unconcerned about anything that is not the divine will, realising—as the commentary of Mgr F. Vincent has clearly demonstrated[19]—that this will is the will of a Father who cares for the welfare of his children. As for St John of the Cross, although he counsels a transforming passivity in order to escape from the chains of our disordered nature, he also says that after the drama of our death to self there comes a dramatic resurrection; man, the whole man, including the life of our senses, has, for his destiny, a restoration of his true and authentic being.

Contemporary Christianity will never accept a rejection of the temporal values of creation. That is why it is very disturbed by the

[18] Quoted by F. Hermans, *Histoire doctrinale de l'humanisme chrétien*, Tournai & Paris, 1948, vol. 3, p. 97. The same author observes elsewhere: "It is most imprudent to imagine that spiritual writers who speak of the joy to be found in God's grace, are guilty of panhedonism. For this joy exists." He also suggests that we should distinguish between sensible joy and the spiritual peace which results from the love of God (*Mystique*, Paris, 1936, pp. 129, 136).
[19] F. Vincent, *Saint François de Sales, directeur d'âmes*, Paris, 1923. There is, however, one passage, among the letters quoted by Bremond, that is open to discussion. It says: "The pleasure of pleasing God is not strictly the love of God, but only a fruit thereof which a man might separate therefrom like as a lemon from a lemon-tree." Is this quite accurate? The pleasure of pleasing is of course distinct from its object, but when kept separate from that object does it remain entirely the same? Does it not, in fact, degenerate?

idea, found in the old writers, of the devouring love of God that seems to imply contempt for this world. But extremes meet, and if a spiritual writer should reduce God in the mystical experience to a mere prospect of love and a method without content, he would not be so very far distant from a kind of atheist mysticism. Like it he would have succumbed to the illusion of making a division between God and one of his attributes, and would be committed to a *cul-de-sac* through not realising that his terminology was ambiguous.

No human being can renounce the peace that is in God: the saints who pray in the destitution of all light, and the singers whom their Prince has forsaken have in reality the divine presence in their love and in their courage; their being is flooded with a gratitude and a generous self-giving which brings them God's deepest reality. Then again, no one can totally renounce himself: this would really be an impossibility and a contradiction. I may say that I must renounce myself in order that I may love God. But when I turn to God I inevitably find a will that wills my perfection. It is God himself who brings me back to myself. There is a first step when I must leave myself in order to attend to God; there is another step when I must become reconciled with the good self that Another has pointed out to me. So it is the evil self only that has to be cast off, the incubus of disordered nature, the rags of sin.[20] Lastly, contempt for creation and created beings has only a very limited function in true Christian mystics. My love for another does not abolish him nor is it just an opportunity to display my charity. If such were the case, we should be reduced to an impersonal and absurd formality, or at least to something quite foreign to Christianity. In the Christian view, *things* may perhaps be only reflexions and stepping-stones, but *persons* have a destiny that is intrinsic and absolute.

Christianity really rejects all forms of mysticism that imply the annihilation or even the substantial dismissal of oneself and other men. What it demands is only death to selfishness, discipline—that

---

[20] "Myself archtraitor to myself" in the words of an impassioned but balanced poem by Christina G. Rossetti ("Who shall deliver me?"). Self-hatred is the condition for all spiritual life. But which self? Surely not the self that is dissatisfied with itself and has turned wholeheartedly to God.

can be crucifying—in one's self-esteem and in one's relations with others. But to offer the self to God is not, as Simone Weil affirmed, to "de-create" it. W. R. Inge is sounder when he says that that which vanishes on the heights of prayer is in no sense our individuality, at least in the view of Christian mystics, but only the partition walls of our individuality. But Inge adds a most important observation; namely, that persons with a temperament likely to respond to a mystical vocation have, as a rule, a tendency to indulge their senses. Hence the pedagogical necessity to warn them more than other men of the dangers that beset them. It is a fact that those destined to *agape* are usually more "erotic" than others: they have a rich and highly developed sensibility, like artists; and all endowment of a refined sense of discrimination has as its counterpart greater possibilities of egoism and perversion.[21]

We decided above that the knowledge of God and of his action in us was situated in a region of penumbra, midway between darkness and light. We have now reached a similar intermediary idea, or rather a necessary synthesis with regard to the problem of what it is right for us to love. To exclude created beings in order to love the Creator is not in conformity with the religion of the Redeemer; but to exclude the Creator and the Redeemer on the excuse of protecting the world's chances of development and its originality, would be even more monstrous. The truth is that created being only finds its inmost reality when it finds the being of God. For the dialectic of either . . . or, we must substitute another: both . . . and. Rather than a mysticism of radical self-obliteration we should choose that of self-transcendence or of ever-renewed conversion, in which the self is not eliminated but illuminated by God. We have used the word conversion; the issue of *that* is development and not de-creation; the sorting-out of the genuine self willed by God and willed with him; the rejection of the self that is separated from God, which certainly implies a kind of death of the natural will in love with its own limitations, but also a kind of re-birth of the will transfigured by grace. The great mystical tradition of Christianity is represented

[21] W. R. Inge, *Christian Mysticism*, London, 1933, 7th edition, p. 372; *The Philosophy of Plotinus*, London, 1918, vol. 2, p. 158.

at its best in this respect by St Francis of Assisi, whom no one can accuse of lukewarmness or banality. And it was no accident that his theocentrism gave so central a position to Christ, i.e. to the Incarnation. We are very far from having worked out all the consequences of a mysticism of this kind which is ultimately far more balanced than most of the others on which the manuals of spirituality have concentrated since the beginning of this century.

3. What is it Necessary for us to Do?

Christian mysticism moves to God without abandoning the world. According to Bergson, this is what gives it its superiority over the doctrines of world-flight taught in classical Greece or in the East. It may be thought that this judgement is too summary, and in fact it is. Plato's contemplative ideal remained flexible; it was Philo who made it rigid through his contempt for the body, and Plotinus through his contempt for the lower classes of society. With regard to Buddhism, it has produced *bodhisattvas* who renounce their entry into nirvana out of love for their human brethren with whom they wish to remain. But this renunciation is in their eyes a second-best, and Arnold Toynbee has spoken of a "sublime inconsistency" in Buddha himself.[22] With these reservations, Bergson's opinion can be considered right. Christian monks have been able, more extensively and more profoundly than the pagan mystics, to maintain with entire consistency and joy that "to work is to pray". This they could do because of their religion's metaphysical optimism and its call to salvation.

From the point of view of what it effects in the world, prayer in the strict sense is an anticipation of the world finally renewed, not a conclusive achievement; even when it is accompanied by miracles it still retains an uncompleted element, for by definition any miracle is only a partial accomplishment of a far greater work to come, only an instalment of the final order of things when matter will be glorified. But prayer in the strict sense needs to be supplemented; it needs prayer in the wider sense, which is work, or behaviour hallowed by right intention. The whole of life thus becomes activity

[22] A. Toynbee, *An Historian's Approach to Religion*, Oxford, 1956, p. 64.

inspired by contemplation. The precept to pray without ceasing "means envisaging the whole of the saint's life as one great prayer in which what we ordinarily call prayer forms only a part".[23] The French school of spirituality, whose limitations we have admitted, at least grasped thoroughly this relationship between the contemplative life and action; it affirmed that the Christ whom we begin by holding before our eyes must be transmitted first to the heart and then to the hands: from contemplation to communion, then to cooperation.

This distinction between prayer in the strict and wider sense is a distinct improvement on that between the sacred and the profane in the programme of our activities. But what proportion must be assigned to each? It is here that the Christian religion shows its originality. First of all, it claims that all things are already accomplished in Jesus Christ, since our prayers in their transmission through him are absolutely sure of being heard. His redemptive incarnation protects us from all frustration in the prayers we make as individuals; their answer has its first fruits in him. Secondly, there is a communion of saints in the Church. Consequently, particular callings do no radical harm to the balance of the whole and never involve absolute frustration for anyone. In the Church, for example, there are Orders that are contemplative and Orders that are active; what the one type cannot do, the other can, but they all form the one Body; they collaborate in the same work and receive the same life. Each can be satisfied with his lot. The lowest place is often even the most necessary; what, for instance, would become of the choir monks if there were no lay brothers? Eating is an indispensable preliminary to chanting. It is true, of course, that such invisible honour must lead to visible suffering—and the gaining of much merit. It can happen that the splendours of the theory may serve to create or maintain a *de facto* distribution of work which is unjust or stupid. It

[23] A. Hamman, *Prières des premiers chrétiens*, Paris, 1952, p. 377. The gospel stresses the danger of keeping to prayer in words only. It asks for guarantees of its authenticity, fasting, for example. This is a further aspect of the problem of contemplation and action and a most formidable aspect in view of our lukewarmness and superficiality.

can happen that superiors are a little too ready to appeal to supernatural motives in order to silence the discontented; it is convenient and inadequate. Abuses exist and men can mishandle the truth. For all that, they do not do away with it, and it saves men from despair. It remains when all else collapses.

A further aspect of the same doctrine is the fact that we can contemplate and serve Christ in others, and especially in the unfortunate. Through this, the whole realm of activity comes to be incorporated in prayer and to be hallowed. This is an idea originating in the gospel and is a central teaching of Matthew 25. The verdict of the last judgement will be based on this alone: "I was hungry, and you gave me food, thirsty, and you gave me drink; I was a stranger and you brought me home, naked and you clothed me, sick and you cared for me, a prisoner, and you came to me." To the surprise of both the elect and the reprobate, Christ answers their questions as to the meaning of this, by simply saying: "Believe me, when you did it to one of the least of my brethren here, you did it to me." This is an echo of Isaiah's words: "Do not turn your back on him who is your brother", but the whole outlook has been given a wonderful new meaning through the identification of the brother with Christ. Christ's presence, however, remains hidden until the day of judgement; a proof that he does not take the place of the unfortunate as though they were nothing but an opportunity or pretext for the practice of charity. This is not an isolated passage in the Synoptics, and it is *a fortiori* in agreement with the teaching of St John. It is, therefore, all the more astonishing that it has not given rise to a vigorous school of spirituality in the Church, but the fact is that only St John of God has worked out a body of teaching based upon it. Taking an even wider view, ought we not to seek God in every event and in all our work and duties? This would completely expose the opposition between Christian piety and all forms of flight from cosmic responsibilities.

This point is so essential that we must conclude by giving it some attention. Theology has of course abundantly developed the idea of Christ's presence in the Church. But it seems to have been much less concerned to give a positive account of another mode of the presence

of Jesus, a presence not in the Church as such, but more fundamentally in the whole human race, and especially in its afflicted members.
The gospel tells us not only about the first presence, but also about
the second. And the second itself is twofold: Christ is present in
those unfortunates who are pure in heart, he is also present in all
who are wretched, quite apart from their moral stature; to the
extent to which a human being is weak or persecuted a Christian will
hold him sacred. This was an idea not unknown to pagan antiquity,
but in the gospel narratives it has a disturbing and stimulating
prominence. We need only remember the parable of the rich man
and Lazarus.

It is true that in the judgement scene discussed above Jesus only
describes himself to the Gentiles as being present in persecuted
believers: the sorting would therefore take place on the issue of the
works of mercy that had or had not been performed with regard to
Christians. But the reader feels at once that the expression "one of the
least of my brethren here" has universal overtones. An interpretation which did not go further than the frontiers of the actually
existing Church would fail to give its full meaning to this last public
instruction given by Christ before his Passion, and would even
falsify it. Every man is a potential Christian, for Christ is calling him
to himself, and in his own person all men are included.

It would, of course, be possible to try to reduce a verse such as the
following: "Whoever gives you a cup of water to drink because you
are Christ's, that man, believe me, shall not lose his reward" (Mark
9. 41), to a narrow meaning of exclusive reference to the Church.
But the wider outlook becomes immediately evident if we compare
the different passages that refer to the little child whom Christ
causes to come and stand in the middle of his disciples. In one of the
passages we read: "Unless you become like little children, you will
not enter the kingdom of heaven" (Mat. 18. 3); and in the other:
"Whoever in my name welcomes one such child, welcomes me"
(Mark 9. 37). In this last passage, Christ's presence is definitely in
the child itself and is distinct from his presence in the group of his
disciples.

Research is needed in order to follow the theme of the twofold

presence of Christ (in the Church and in mankind as a whole) as it
was developed by the Fathers. Origen has preserved the following
logion. "And Jesus said: For the sake of the weak, I became weak;
because of the hungry, I hungered; because of the thirsty, I
thirsted." St Hilary even dared to affirm that the body Christ made
his own contained all mankind. "By this union of all men in Himself, He is like a city, and by our union with His flesh we are the
inhabitants". St John Chrysostom returns again and again in his
sermons to the judgement scene in Matthew. "He it is whòm we
despise in the poor; hence the enormity of the crime." Do not
decorate churches, if that means neglecting the poor. The latter
temple is more august than the former. St Augustine: "Christ's
whole body groans in pain. Until the end of the world, when pain
will pass away, this man groans and cries to God. . . . Thus there is
but one man who reaches unto the end of time, and those that cry
are always His members." Or again: "Christ is himself evangelised;
he is evangelised even in his members who already exist, in order
to bring others, and that those who were not his members, may come
and be united to them."

Nor did the Scholastics overlook this idea. St Thomas affirms
that Christ is the head not only of the saints in heaven or of believers on earth, but of all men "who as yet are only potentially
united to him" in belief, even though they may never become so.
And Cajetan comments: "Christ has taken in Himself all suffering,
in order to divinise all the ills of the universe."[24]

Christian tradition has thus believed that Christ is in all mankind
or that all mankind is in Christ. It has sometimes been tempted to
interpret the words of the New Testament in a narrow sense:
Origen, for example, seems to limit Christ's presence to believers:

[24] For all these texts from the Fathers and Scholastics I refer the reader to
E. Mersch, *The Whole Christ.* The Historical Development of the Doctrine of
the Mystical Body in Scripture and Tradition, London, 1949, pp. 293, 331–2,
423, 457–8, 466. I have added to them a text from St Augustine, *Enarrationes in
Ps.* 74, in Migne, PL, 36, col. 949.
    Note also this text of the Council of Quiersy in 853: "*Christus Iesus D. N.,
sicut nullus homo est, fuit vel erit, cuius natura in illo assumpta non fuerit, ita nullus
est, fuit vel erit homo, pro quo passus non fuerit; licet non omnes passionis eius
mysterio redimantur.*" Denzinger, *Enchiridion Symbolorum,* 319.

"In each of the saints who are sick," he says with reference to Matthew 25.[25] It is only an apparent limitation, however, for the basic affirmation is that man has an immense dignity due to his religious vocation. The brotherhood of man is universal, it gains unsuspected depth from the fact that the Redemption has given new force not only to its demands but also to its potentialities. Moreover, in the view of St Augustine and other Fathers, the Church began with Abel: it is co-extensive with human history.[26] But Christ is present in different degrees and modes. In scholastic terminology his presence is sometimes in act and sometimes in potency, or in St Augustine's more metaphorical words, Christ himself approaches himself (in men), he prays and is prayed to, diversely.

In our time we might devote ourselves to developing these ideas and express the spirit of the New Testament in a different form by saying that Christ is in men sometimes as a beggar, sometimes as a donor. In mankind as a whole (whether baptised or not) he is present in order to question and to call to us; in the Church he is present in order to give his own answer to that question, i.e. to reveal and save. On the one hand, he is at the basis of the suffering of the unfortunate, or, more objectively, in every just cause that is weak and persecuted; on the other, he is in his members who have accepted the message of salvation and must carry it to the world. Thus, among men, Jesus answers himself by means of the Christians. This is the profound meaning of the prayer he utters and of the action he inspires. If this is true, it means that Christian prayer is incorporated in a divine movement. And what it requires of us is perhaps the opposite of that which we are ordinarily led to do. It is much less a question of asking some favour from God than of listening to him and of responding to him in union with the Spirit he bestows on us by his Son.

This kind of divine circulation in human history repeats on the plane of revelation a process that is universal in religious life. For God's answer to human petition, reaching us through events and

---

[25] A. Hamman, op. cit., p. 375.
[26] Y. Congar, "Peut-on définir l'Eglise?", in *Jacques Leclerq: L'Homme, l'œuvre et ses amis*, Paris, 1961, p. 238.

even sin, is often a counter-prayer which he makes to us. He awakens a new need in our soul, not only as a reply, but as the further prayer which we are to make our own; our future self, with its structure completed, will be produced in this way through grace. The details are difficult to perceive, but we take part in this way in the genesis and assimilation of the creative word in the listening servant: he becomes God's child. As he prays, his being is harmonised and lifted up. Something of his first questioning remains, but something is destroyed too, and, lastly, something new is born.

Parallel with this development there is another, that of our ideas about God himself: the clash between our nature and his reality lessens. Is this not the normal course of spiritual education? We first pray to the God of nature, we even thank him for having enriched us with the spoils of this world, "like the frank and bloody child of an ogress". But the God of the moral order moves us to do good with the riches of iniquity. And when we promise to reform ourselves, we are led to transform our original, childish notion of the divine power, precisely in order that we may acknowledge the unity of God's countenances as expressed both in external reality and in the depth of our spirit. Our idea of God becomes purified in the measure in which our idea of ourselves and the world is purified.[27]

If we now return to Christian prayer, we observe that the ultimate source of the whole spiritual dialectic has a name of his own: it is the Logos who prays to the Father in us, and who prays to us in mankind in order that we may pray with him to the Father in the Spirit. Thus the final synthesis of all the forms of prayer which we have examined, is achieved. For, in its full significance, prayer addressed to men is already sacred and we find ourselves associated with nothing less than the divine prayer itself in a Trinitarian mystery. The prayer each of us makes to the best element of himself, then that which binds men together in an immense drama of inter-related expression, leads us in fact far beyond what we

[27] A film by Fernandel, *Ali Baba and the Forty Thieves*, illustrates in an amusing and perhaps unconscious way this hidden development of prayer. Man is caught in the snare of his religion, but it is for his own good—and for that of his religion!

imagined. We join up with the prayer God addresses to himself through created beings. And beyond this divine action in time we have a glimpse of God's inner life in eternity: a life in which prayer is still present but has no other purpose than the mysterious love of the uncreated Persons and the gathering together of all things in them.

Note on Vocal Prayer
and the Mystics

Plotinus taught that we "should invoke God himself, not by words, but by an aspiration of our soul to prayer; this is the way in which we can pray to him alone with the alone".[1] The philosopher did not deny the usefulness of vocal prayer, but he reduced it to the level of a natural activity. It has no power to reach God, it extends only to beings of this world—that includes the stars within it—and acts upon them in a magical fashion and unknown to them, in the same way as we ourselves receive their influence; in short, it is irrational and an incantation: "Prayer produces its effects because one part of the universe is in sympathy with another, just as in the tense string of a lyre a vibration from below travels upwards." "Contemplation alone is free of all spell-like quality."[2]

The transcendence of the One is thus in liaison with the dumbness of his worshippers. Now it is absolutely certain that every deeply religious attitude eventually, in some way or other, ends in silence. The Old Testament provides examples of awed silence or of men reduced to stammering in face of the grandeur of Yahweh. The fact that it was forbidden to pronounce the name of Yahweh involved a religious break in the flow of speech; from this fact alone language was shown to be inadequate and to point beyond itself.

But extremes meet. Would not the constant repetition of the divine name, and it alone, make vocal prayer the best introduction to contemplation? Many Easterners thought so, and among Christians the hesychast monks were convinced of it. St John Climacus advised: "Let the name of Jesus be fused with your breathing"; Nicephorus taught that the petition: "Lord Jesus Christ, have

[1] *Enneads*, 5, 1, 6.
[2] Ibid., 8, 4, 41 and 44. Cf. R. Arnou, *Le Désir de Dieu dans la philosophie de Plotin*, Paris, n.d., pp. 49–50.

mercy on me", should be endlessly repeated. Flooded by this single thought, a monk would be disposing himself for the vision of the divine light. Through this invocation, which involved both the tongue and the ear, the whole organism became suited to see God.[3] But since God is invisible and free in his essence, will not this vision, however vivid, be a vision of a divine "energy"[4] rather than of God himself? Hesychasm gave rise to the synthesis worked out by Gregory Palamas, and from this synthesis sprang the Palamite and Antipalamite quarrel that troubled the Greek Church for centuries.

When we approach each other in human prayer and when we pray to God, the proper name fills the role of silence: it precedes any explicit petition. It is a void aspiring to be filled; it fosters the production of any number of insights, images and emotions. It disposes us to welcome what the other has to say, and awakens us to new awareness. Herein lies the power of litanies and of those brief exclamations that are inseparable from all dialogue between persons. In the spiritual life, invocation of this kind is all the more necessary in that the advent of this word prevents silence sliding into sleep. The distance between God and man proves exhausting to man. The body must come to the rescue of the spirit and prevent mental prayer from becoming chaotic. (Try to be an angel and you become a beast . . .) No religion exists that does not practise this repeated appeal, made simply, with the divine name; and this is wisdom.

Nevertheless, the proper name and the litany can also be ambi-

---

[3] *Dictionnaire de Théologie catholique*, article "Palamas", col. 1752. This spiritual training is linked with a curious notion of anatomy and physiology, and to an equally debatable idea of the divine vision. But it also includes a profound doctrine of the Orthodox tradition: its belief in the Risen Christ. It was through always looking to the conclusion of a Christian's divinisation in Christ and to the transformation in the cosmos which results from it, that Byzantine spirituality came to appear as, fundamentally, *vision*. This scandalised the Latins, but if we forget it, we shall not understand much about the hesychasts, or even perhaps about Pseudo-Dionysius.

[4] [The Greek theologians held that God is unknowable in his *essence*, but that he has revealed himself to us in his *energies*. These latter are "God himself" in his action and revelation to the world. God exists complete and entire in each of his energies. Cf. Timothy Ware, *The Orthodox Church*, London, Penguin Books, 1963, p. 77. This book gives an excellent account of the hesychasts, Palamas, etc.—*Translator*.]

guous auxiliaries. Instead of being a void aspiring to be filled, they can reverse the position and present themselves as fullness itself. That is why vocal prayer may not be reduced to itself alone. Vocal prayer must also express itself in connected speech and do its best to make its content explicit. Prayer builds up a body for itself, and that is natural. It incorporates its aspirations in established prayers that are normative both for the individual and the group.

In Christianity, there is an additional reason for this procedure which arises from revelation. For Christian prayer is based upon the word of God; it derives its nourishment from the Scriptures and becomes liturgical prayer. It is vocal and it adopts fixed forms for a reason that springs not only from psychological need and moral weakness, but from the intrinsic inspiration of the faith.

We must worship in spirit and in truth, and the last word must be assigned to spirit. The word my lips transmit suffers from my own sluggishness. The danger is, and we all know this from experience, that it may become mechanical. There is also the danger of our becoming advocates, of our justifying ourselves to God, whereas we should do better by simply being ourselves in his presence. This is why vocal prayer which is a necessity both for mysticism and for the liturgy, must be intermediate and subordinate. Piety must always keep control of its forms of expression; it cannot exclude fixed forms, but neither can it confine prayer to a series of words that hold good for everyone in all circumstances.

Sound sense allows that vocal prayer is indispensable, but affirms that it must be kept within bounds. Our conclusion therefore is not one of startling novelty. Still it deserves attention, for it contains the paradox of these contraries: the soul needs the body, the spirit needs the letter. A principle is superior, only if it can convert its enemies into friends, and this possibility of reconciliation is inherent in all things as the condition of their salvation.

Epilogue

Of what use is it to pray? This is a typically Western question; we look for utility and are engrossed, sometimes in a miserly way, with the end and the means. Easterners are often impatient at our lack of the contemplative spirit. In their view, prayer is an end in itself. It belongs to a realm of expression that contains in itself its own value.[1] Artists, philosophers, mystics all understand this language, and we have taken their evidence.

The polarity that exists in the constitution of the infra-human world is a sign or prefigurement of the dialogue between conscious beings. This mutuality—without which there would be neither persons nor society of persons, or, indeed, anything at all—has its perfect manifestation in prayer. Prayer, that is to say, first of all as a relationship between human beings themselves, and, then, even more importantly, in their relationship with God. No doubt it is true that there is no knowledge of God and no consciousness of duty to him that is not discerned through the aid of *ea quae facta sunt*; but it is no less true that human intercourse is stunted and stifled if men do not find the originating principle of their personalities in a source higher than themselves. Without this vital drive towards God, the human condition rapidly becomes pointless and unstable, and without love among men the worship of God becomes puerile or hateful.

For this reason, the two parts of this enquiry cannot be divorced. It is futile to try to separate our approach to God from our approach to man, or, in the terminology of spiritual writers, to separate "prophetic" from "mystical" devotion, Benedictine contemplation from Ignatian ascetism, or the theocentric outloook from humanism.

---

[1] Cf. T. Ohm, *Die Gebetsgebärden der Völker und das Christentum*, Leiden, 1948, p. 21.

For each of these series degenerates when it claims independence from the other.[2]

Recourse to prayer does not produce an automatic reward, and we have frequently pointed out its possible distortions. But at the wellhead, if not always throughout its course, prayer is good. On the human level it is one of the indispensable bonds of human relationships; it is a privileged approach road to ourselves and to others. Sometimes it is the means to freedom, sometimes its result. The influence exerted by one person on another through prayer is always transmitted through the autonomy of the one and received through the autonomy of the other. When a man comes to me as a suppliant, I take up his petition and present it to myself; I answer myself when I answer him. The other man's prayer provokes this prayer to myself which is a development of my being. The new factor, the result of the petition, is only produced through its reiteration and integration in the person of the recipient.[3]

A similar process occurs on the religious plane. To the extent to which prayer takes place from man to God and from God to man, man acquires his true stature and freedom. The religious man knows this from experience. He knows that in union with God his true self begins to be and to develop; he even suspects that were there no divine transcendence there would be no possibility of speaking of a human thou. But God has willed that this situation which is ours should in a sense become *his* through the Incarnation. Therefore,

[2] See on this point some excellent remarks by K. E. Kirk, *The Vision of God*, pp. 450–1.

[3] These ideas are presented in the following terms in a letter I have received from F. De Beer: "To pray is an act I have to force myself to perform: it can require much of me, humiliate me, etc. I have to *call* upon all that is best in me (perhaps, though, no exercise of the will and of the memory is separable from some kind of reverence for oneself). But above all, when I address a prayer to someone else, I do not expect an immediate, quasi-automatic answer. The other person has to address to himself the prayer I have made him. *Any given prayer, therefore, implies at the least three prayers.*" In this sense, "prayer to oneself is an essential element in all prayer." I am particularly happy to welcome this suggestion because it seems to me to prolong in a striking and independent way the division of the consciousness into the ideal self and the positive self, and, further, the coincidence of the ideal self and the thou of which I had outlined a description in *Vers la Philosophie de l'amour et de la personne*, Paris, 1957, pp. 121–34.

from a Christian point of view, prayer discloses one of the ultimate secrets of being which from person to person in freedom and love sweeps through heaven and earth.

Freedom only becomes significant through love, and to pray always involves entrusting oneself to the person to whom one prays. It is an admission that it is impossible to live or act with full intensity and truth without him. On the religious plane this means that the capacity for mutual relationship is now directed to the grace of God who draws us to share in his divinity. Even the grace that God creates in us is destined to introduce us to his presence and to his inmost reality. We become in a sense unable to tolerate his absence or do anything practical for him or for ourselves without his help.[4] The "passivity" of the mystics is simply the expression of the conviction, resulting from unquestionable experience, that man does not conquer God, but is himself laid hold of, penetrated and renewed by him; passivity is simply another name for the fullest activity, one that is beyond all expectation.

In the mystical life, a man realises that that life springs up spontaneously and at the same time comes down from God. In it the connexion between the created autonomy and the creative act is more intimate and more fully appreciated than in ordinary religious experience. But even in such ordinary experience, and even in its rudimentary forms, we are made to realise that earth and heaven cannot be severed. This is a constant factor which applies both to the individual consciousness and to corporate relationships. Our whole examination of this matter has verified a fact which we suggested at the start, namely, that the content and form of what men seek from each other in a given civilisation is affected by the content and form of that which they seek from heaven, and *vice versa*.

At the same time—and this is a second fact which is no less

---

[4] Therefore, a prayer which—even if couched in the form of a petition—took no account of this essential attitude of expectancy would be both contradictory and ridiculous (like, for example, the invocation: "Sacred Heart of Jesus, have trust in me"). The saints knew their frailty. Philip Neri used to say: "Lord, look after me, for I shall betray thee and do all manner of evil, if thou help me not" (quoted by I. Ponnelle and L. Bordet, *Saint Philippe Néri et la société romaine de son temps*, Paris, 1929, p. 532).

interesting—the two prayers are not identical. The dialogue between men springs from their vital needs; it is directed to a human partner, it continues along the essential lines of its own development before it begins to show up what God (or what absence of God) is implied in the concrete encounters in which we are engaging. In a parallel way, the conversations of the believer on Sinai do not immediately reflect the words that he will speak with his brothers on the plain. It resembles the two poles of an ellipse; only little by little do their axes attract each other and end in meeting.

They will only meet, however, provided that their field of action has not been sullied. If one of the poles has been thus desecrated, then sooner or later the other will suffer in the same way. In this respect, our epoch is confronted by a choice of paramount importance that will decide the fate of mankind, and the precise object of this choice is prayer. The chief danger that threatens to impoverish mankind is not only the fact that men are ceasing to raise their hands in prayer to God; it is also the fact that they are ceasing to regard the human individual as a sacred being. The first threat is so obvious that we need not dwell on it. The second is more insidious and justifies our raising the alarm. We are taking part in a vast massacre of those natural sacraments which fertilised all earlier civilisations and we are on the way to de-humanising ourselves. The evil does not lie in the fact that our science is objective and is ridding phenomena of those subjective fantasies which our ancestors had incorporated in them. For true science always develops in wonder; it goes ever deeper into the splendours and the inalienable laws of a hidden harmony. The evil lies, rather, in the hardening produced by the techniques made possible by science. The evil lies, ultimately, in ourselves who make use of these techniques; it lies in that accumulated guilt which insinuates itself within us, so drugging us that we become unaware of our degradation. Shall we prove capable of liberating ourselves from the worship of our own productions? Shall we count nothing valuable save in so far as it contributes to material and social advancement? Shall we seal ourselves off in our own self-sufficiency? Or, shall we take the opposite direction and prove capable of allowing beauty to blossom once again in our hands? Shall we learn to respect the deep reality which is the source of our freedom? Shall we become willing to welcome a message that will make us more self-exacting and open to the uniqueness of other people?

It may seem that the response we ask for does not amount to much. The worship of the beautiful, the true and the good as it exists in the individual and in his relationship with others would seem to be a form of religiosity that is vague indeed. And so it is. It would only let in a little fresh air upon a torpid world. It would be a small matter, wholly insufficient to fill the programme of prayer. But if even this proved too difficult for our times, then we should infallibly lose, together with the divine dialogue, the human dialogue which it claimed to maintain and direct. The "world of the vocative" might continue in appearance, and even develop in excited talk and superficial conformism. But in this inflated emptiness the give and take of really human intercourse would lose all its substance and lead to spiritual numbness. The loss of prayer would mean the loss of the person.

It has always been true that the pattern of our relationships with others is by nature transitory and changeable; it dissolves into anonymous ideas and images, the products of its disintegration. Still, these can be used again later as the materials for a renewed integration. Each of us builds himself and builds his world of relationships with others and with God according to this twofold movement whose risks are made evident by, and whose mystery is contained in, the existence of language.

But mankind, through a silent revolution, of which most philosophers even are still unaware, is, in this century, in process of creating a new language, a mathematical language, whose flexibility will enable it to express and to direct life, including personal life, with a power and subtility, compared with which the Cartesian *Organon* appears as a crude sketch. What services and threats such an instrument brings with it, an instrument that is able to insinuate itself not only into the structure of matter, but into the varied interplay of organisms and social life, on so many levels and in so many spheres! What surprises it has in store for us! This is a final reason, and not the least, for raising the alarm on behalf of prayer. Mankind is exposed, as never before, to the temptation to hurl itself into the objective calculation of subjective reality. That calculation is admirable and operative. But the loftiest ranges of the human person and of his relationship with others lie elsewhere: these are expressed in an invocation that can alone explore and bring to limitless perfection the "same" and the "different", that can alone pass from the *logos* which is a calculating function to the *logos* which brings into being the whole sphere of intelligent and loving mutuality between human minds and hearts. This is why today more than yesterday, tomorrow more than today, the prayer of mankind will decide its history.